CONTENTS

FLICKING THROUGH THIS BOOK, I'm sure anyone would be inspired by the range and strength of Argentina's diverse groups resisting oppression and creating alternative's to neoliberalism and economic globalisation. As well as this, for me the discovery of Argentina's resistance and struggle for autonomy meant, for the first time, a connection rather than a rejection of the country.

There were lots of reasons for my rejection or disinterest in Argentina. These included my intermittently difficult relationship with my Argentinian mum, and teasing at school, mainly about Maradona's hand of god, but also about the Falklands War. Two visits to see my family in Argentina after the dictatorship had ended in1983 were also important factors. As a short-haired, trouser wearing opinionated teenager, I struggled with a middle-class family who seemed to want to deny the existence of severe inequalities and poverty in Argentina.

Twelve years had passed since my last visit, for most of which I took no interest in the country apart from occasional news from the family or my mum returning with big pots of *Dulce de Leche* — Argentina's national dessert. The events of December 2001 took me by surprise, I'm not sure if that was due to lack of information available prior to the uprising or my denial of my Argentinian roots. Soon there was information overload, *piqueteros, cacerolazos, escraches, asambleas*. My mates would ask me what I knew about what was happening and I would have to admit shamefully that I knew little. My family had been asking for about ten years why I hadn't been to see them, my grandad got ill and the politics got more and more interesting. It felt like the time was right to go back.

The time I spent in Argentina was incredibly intense. On the one hand, I felt unconditionally welcomed by *MOCASE* (a *campesino* human rights group) who after we arrived almost unannounced treated us like family and wanted to share their story and struggle and very limited sleeping space! On the other hand, I felt very uncomfortable when I visited the houses of middle class family friends who had Nestlé-laden fridges and maids and lived very comfortably despite the country's economic crisis (admittedly many of them were involved in local assemblies or neighbourhood soup kitchens). Argentina is, and always has been, a country of insupportable contrasts.

As I learnt about the current struggles and more about the history of the country, especially the dirty wars and the guerrilla movements of the 1970s, Argentina became a new country. On the *escrache,* I was caught off guard. I had gone with reservations about being voyeuristic: watching someone else's struggle rather than doing it yourself. But as I joined in with the singing, I was filled with anger towards the military, the detention centres, the torture, and memories of my uncle in law who was murdered by the Triple A. I remembered the quiet Argentinian friends who used to come to our house in London, and my mum trying to explain to her inquisitive seven year old daughter, that they'd been in prison not because they had done anything wrong but because there were some bad people in their government. I no longer felt on the outside. I felt a strong link with their history and their struggle.

During the three months I was in Argentina, I met lots of incredible people struggling, resisting and surviving, and saw inspiring pockets of autonomy and self-management; I found a part of Argentina that I never knew existed, an Argentina with which I now feel a strong connection.

Tash December 2003

Arriving in Argentina, its 'Europeaness' took me by surprise — the language with its Italian inflection, its Parisian architecture, its cold winter reminding me of the grey English weather. Although I was on the other side of the world, and in a different hemisphere I felt at home. I was eager to learn from the *piqueteros*, the unemployed workers, the café owners, the *cartoneros* collecting cardboard, everyone. I wanted to know what lessons they could teach me from the crisis of 2001 when they organised themselves, took on the policies of the state, the military and the world's financial institutions, threw out their government, and become famous the world over for autonomous politics.

I wasn't disappointed. At every corner, I found inspiration. Over a mate (the country's national drink) people were willing to share their ideas, their politics, their hopes for the future. The desire for autonomy and change was everywhere. Recently

vacated banks had been turned into centres for neighbourhood assemblies, decaying Spanish villas had been reused by squatters, even street corners had been transformed into meeting places. A huge shipbuilders yard which we visited soon after our arrival was used to host a national assembly for unemployed groups. Thousands came to sell their products, to share stories, to cook and to organise. In the rural north, MOCASE were helping other farmers organise, know their rights and build a co-operative economy after years of subjugation by local strong-arm *caudillos*.

We encountered a demonstration nearly everyday, always numbering tens of thousands. In the biting cold of the southern hemisphere winter, people gathered to demand an end to impunity for the military leaders, for more food and work, and for the right to protest. There was an outpouring of popular democracy and creativity. The energy was contagious. Such desire for far-reaching change and to control your own life and community is understandable in a country brought to its knees so often and so desperately. As one woman told me: 'there's no way we can go back now, back to our old way of life. We've struggled and we've organised for ourselves. We've made bread, our own houses and we've laughed and sang. And we're winning. We don't need any of them — the bosses and politicians. We've got a saying round here — get rid of them all'.

Paul January 2004

Mountain High Maps ® Copyright ©1993 Digital Wisdom, Inc.

"Sometimes the things we do seem so small, like making our own bread, setting up an after-school kids club, learning about our own health, or protesting in the street. But together, we're creating a new way of life beyond the control of the bosses and politicians who have oppressed and exploited us. We're taking back control."

DECEMBER 2001 IN ARGENTINA represented one of those exciting glimpses of revolutionary fervour. Not a revolution of Marxist-Leninists, or trade unions, or party politicians. But a popular revolution when many different groups joined together. People were more or less united in getting rid of political leaders and bosses who denied to the majority of Argentinians access to a decent quality of life. However briefly, the working class piqueteros (the road blockers) were joined by the more middle class carceroleros (part of the colourful and noisy Latin American tradition of taking to the streets to demonstrate by banging pots, creating what is known as the carcerolazo) and ahorristas (those who had lost their life savings) to create a dynamite combination which brought down a government. The self-organising which multiplied after this created an insatiable appetite for popular power which still lingers today. 2001 was only a minute in history. But what happened has links in the past and will go on into the future. It is a minute which leapt around the world and inspired millions of people.

There are lots of stories that could be told about what happened in Argentina since 2001. What we have chosen to do here is reflect on the possibilities for autonomy, self-management, people-power. We have chosen this focus mainly because in our time there in 2003 we were inspired by the popular struggles for autonomy, community self-management, or as many people call it, being horizontal. For us in the rich west, there is lots to learn, and lots to listen to. Clearly no one has all the answers and Argentina is a very different place to Europe. Although it has close links with Europe, it still oozes a passionate and chaotic Latin Americanness. But, to spend time with so many groups and individuals on the streets constantly talking about autonomy, taking back their lives from politicians and business leaders they long ago stopped believing in, not waiting for answers to come from someone else, but getting on with creating their own society, is amazingly empowering and something that we have lost sight of in the rich West.

In this book, we bring together stories and experiences of autonomy which form part of Argentina's popular uprising. To start, we discuss some background history to unravel what caused the crisis and what actually happened leading up to, and on, December 2001. Then we discuss some of the autonomous groups — the *piquetero* movement, the unemployed workers movements, neighbourhood assemblies, Independent Media Centres, groups working for justice and human rights such as HIJOS and the Madres de Plaza de Mayo, the struggle of indigenous farmers groups, squatted social centres, reclaimed factories, and experimental spaces and collectives. We also include a number of interviews and reports from actions, events and demonstrations. What follows doesn't cover all those involved in the popular uprising that is remaking politics in Argentina. But we hope these amazing stories of autonomy inspire you as they inspired us.

ARGENTINA A HISTORY OF PLUNDER AND INSUPPRESSIBLE REVOLT

AMID THE ECONOMIC CRISES and political upheavals of the last few decades, Argentina is a country that joins the growing list of casualties alongside the likes of Thailand, Russia and Indonesia. Crippling debt and structural adjustment, de-industrialisation and rocketing unemployment, rampant political corruption and the swindling of the country's resources, military and police personnel acting with impunity as it slaughters its own citizens, US strong-arm intervention, and privatisation which has stripped the country down to its last cent. For Argentina, the list goes on and reads like an nventory of the greatest tragedies and follies of modern day capitalism.

Argentina's unfortunate story, then, is also a story about the madness of the global economy. Argentina was dragged through the same loss of industry and soaring unemployment as other rich countries in the great depression of the 1930s and again in the 1970s. But debt, privatisation, corruption and its lowly place in the global pecking order weakens its ability to respond. In 2002, official unemployment and sub-employment nationally was around 34 per cent. The International Monetary Fund (IMF) is one of the architects of the present madness. While it blames previous military generals for squandering $150 billion in loans which it lent to the country, today's government blames the IMF for irresponsibly lending money to military dictators. Whoever is to blame for past errors, Argentina has lost control of its economy due to conditions on IMF loans and national and international elites acting in the interests of profit. National economies, people's livelihoods and whole neighbourhoods continue to be changed or destroyed at the stroke of pen or a keyboard in decisions made at the world's centres of power in London, New York, Geneva, Washington, and in the case of Argentina, Paris and Madrid as well. Enter also the response: people who say *ya basta* (enough is enough) and *que se vayan todos* (get rid of them all) and are unpicking this madness and building another world in their neighbourhoods, workplaces and homes.

In the face of violence and hardship, unemployment and hunger, most people can only take so much. At some point they say 'enough'. It is these times that we are interested in here, when sufficient people say enough together and take the situation into their own hands. Argentina is no stranger to conflict and popular uprisings. Kicking out President De La Rua in December 2001 is only one example of popular rebellion and desire for autonomy in Argentina's rocky history. The *Semana Trágica* (Tragic Week) in 1919 saw bloody battles between striking workers and the state in Buenos Aires. After a general strike, police repression left 700 dead and 4,000 injured. In the 1960s, popular uprisings such as the '*Cordobazo*' in 1969 saw students and workers clash bloodily with the army in Cordoba, and met bloody responses from a string of violent and repressive governments in the 1970s. Lopez Vega in particular, the key political figure after Peron's death in 1974, organised the notorious 'Triple A' (Anti-Communist Alliance) to combat what they saw as dangerous trade unionists and guerrilla groups such as the Montoneros. In 1976, Argentina entered the most bloody period of its history. Between 1976 to 1983 a series of ruthless military dictators — Videla, Viola, Galtieri — embarked upon the dirty war '*la guerra sucia*' in which 35,000 people were 'disappeared'. Black Ford Falcons driven by the state's secret service cruised the streets of Buenos Aires, filling ordinary citizens with a fear most of us have never experienced. This period remains a shame to most Argentinians, unaccounted for, and a source of impunity. But it also gave birth to a range of human rights groups demanding justice.

'El City'
*Corporate skyscrapers line the
waterfront in Buenos Aires'
gleaming business district*

ARGENTINA
MANY COUNTRIES IN ONE

A STRIKING FEATURE OF ARGENTINA is the remarkable gap between Buenos Aires and the 'provinces'. A journey from *el city* the financial district of Buenos Aires to Jujuy near the Bolivian border, for example, reveals two countries in one — the former a chic and bustling centre in the global capitalist economy, the latter marked by poverty and misery, especially amongst the indigenous groups here. On the fringes of the country, capitalism hardly arrived and was always controlled by semi-feudal local lords — the caudillos. This divide runs deep in Argentinian history between the more liberal 'unitarists' of Buenos Aires who looked towards Europe and wanted to centralise power, and the more conservative 'federalists' of the provinces made up of large landholders and the rural poor who wanted provincial autonomy.

These days, scratch the surface and it's not hard to uncover the often racist and arrogant attitude of the Porteños (the people of Buenos Aires) towards people in the rest of the country. Deep prejudice marks conversations about the 'poor' and 'wretched' in the provinces — where people are poor and backward through lack of education and culture. The criollos are particularly singled out for their lack of (European) culture. Colonialism, institutional racism, uneven development and exploitation clearly don't figure in conversations about why many people are trapped in poverty.

The growth of the notorious *villas miserias* (literally miserable towns, or what we call ghettos or shanty towns) has become an easy metaphor for the country's problems. We are familiar with these places through images on TV — strings of temporary houses on squatted land on the edge of cities, housing migrant workers and cobbled together from wood and tin. In many cases they have become permanent, gaining rights to land and infrastructure such as water and electricity. For some they are a source of hope as an example of self-organisation. Many people are proud to come from there and proud of the way they and their neighbours are coping. Land seizures and land

Villas Miserias

Left, villas line many motorways in Argentina's big cities. A mark of shame for many, they are also places of creativity and self-management, and home to many piqueteros

squatting are a key part of the day to day struggle. In 1983, for example, in the La Matanza area of Greater Buenos Aires 1,200 families who couldn't pay their rent squatted land. They successfully fought-off several evictions, squatted the provincial town hall and blocked roads and eventually through the Law of Expropriation, they were granted permanent tenure. It is in places like this that, today, working class militancy and self organising is the strongest.

But the villas remain a mark of longstanding poverty and government negligence. For middle class society which lacks empathy, they are a mark of the shameful. Most are quick to make a disapproving tut at their mention, but slow to criticise the political corruption and unequal economic game responsible for their existence. The police, on their part, are ready to enter such places, as they did in 2001, to seek out troublemakers, control potential dissent, and shoot tear gas and rubber bullets.

TRYING TO MAKE SENSE OF THE CRISIS

SO HOW DID ARGENTINA get into a mess? Why do people say "enough is enough"? How can a country that has so much potential, natural resources and land have such a troubled history and turbulent present? We've got to take a step back in time.

The answer is not that difficult to find if we look at the usual pattern of exploitation and coloialism which unfolded in Argentina. Colonial rulers — mainly British and Spanish — were the culprits here, exploiting the country's resources and workers and keeping Argentina 'in its place' in the global pecking order. The mostly nomadic indigenous groups who lived in the area at the time were almost wiped out by Old World diseases such as small pox and flu. Most of Argentina's best lands were rapidly monopolised as Spanish immigrants and criollos (Spaniards born in the Americas) began putting vast tracts of it into huge farms called latifundios. It's from these large sheep and cattle estancias that the legendary gauchos riding on the pampas came. In post-independence Argentina from 1816, the picture changed little for the majority. Caudillos (local strong men) emerged in each region which retained much independence, while British investment grew to dominate the Argentinian economy by the 1890s.

So, for much of its history a profit-hungry local, national and global oligarchy, all working in unison have controlled the development of Argentina (as it has done across the third world) and kept the mass of people living on marginal lands or in wage slavery. The country didn't so much develop, as underdevelop. From the start, it got sucked into the global economy on unequal terms and an over-dependency on cash exports such as beef and mutton made it extremely vulnerable.

During the 1940s, the all pervasive influence of the demagogue General Juan Peron, and his party the Justicialists, improved the situation a little for the workers, by bolstering trade unions and securing voting rights for women. While General Peron, and his wife Eva, may have been a shining hope for the working masses, the *descamisadas* (the shirtless ones), he was no revolutionary. Concessions by the Perons weren't focused on worker autonomy or creating a new independent workers movement. They were used, as many times before and since, to contain dissent, to quell the desire for more radical social change — to make the situation bearable and preserve the status quo. Eva's famous handouts to the poor kept them in their place and were not intended to encourage them to find their own solutions to the problems they faced. The prosperous economy of the time, then, afforded some cosmetic changes and gifts to the workers, but only at the price of absolute adherence to the Peron's say.

Eventually, even though he took on the country's oligarchy, he couldn't do anything about Argentina's place in the global pecking order. Left without his wife's charisma after her sudden death in 1952, and bombarded by mounting problems, Peron and his supporters were sent into exile by a military coup in 1955. In the 1960s and 1970s, Argentina swung violently between Peronist and military governments, with General Peron making a brief return to power from 1972–74 before his death. For the large part, economic incompetence and the violence of the military reigned, ending in the Malvinas war, or as they are known in the UK the Falklands. Which brings us to today and the depressingly familiar story of the victory of neoliberal economics and representative democracy — the idea that this is as good as it gets, that TINA (There Is No Alternative) rules. Land, industry, resources, and most of the economy, are given to private foreign firms in the name of free trade and efficiency.

THE POLITICS OF HUNGER AND MISERY

IN THE 1980s AND 1990s, THE BAD TIMES really started. Even though the new UCR government helped the country back to normality after years of military dictatorships, by the time President Alfonsin departed in 1989, Argentina was racked by four-digit annual inflation. Alfonsin had created a new currency, the austral, and their rapid production rate enhanced hyper-inflation. The country was also financially crippled by massive foreign debts.

In such a scene of chaos, the stage was set for the entry of the Peronist President Carlos Menem and his economic minister Cavallo, as Washington's golden boys from 1989–99. Menem set up a currency board which only allowed an increase in money supply when there was an increase in foreign earnings. It was through this that Menem was able to peg the peso to the dollar at a rate of one-to-one. This dollarisation and over-valuation of the peso swelled foreign imports, especially for the rich, but made it costly for local industries to operate. Many small Argentinian firms went to the wall and unemployment continued its upward trajectory.

Menem also set about dismantling the country's vast public sector and virtually all national assets were sold to mainly European investors, who made large profits due to the peso-dollar parity. To the outside world this looked like a good idea to raise a huge amount of cash to pay off Argentina's

Presents of Argentina: left, Leopoldo Galtieri, 1982–83; and right, Carlos Menem, 1989–99

debt. Now let's be clear. Argentina's national companies were nothing to write home about. They were run corruptly and inefficiently and did little to enrich the average Argentinian. Apparently, on Argentinian Airlines for example, 40 per cent of passengers were flying for free as government employees. But what resulted from the big sell off was no better. The companies that emerged — Metrogas, Repsol YPF, Gas Natural, Telefonica, Aguas Argentinas, Edenor, Metrovias, Edesur and Telecom — now make up the bulk of the national energy, utility and transport infrastructure and are all in foreign hands, with profits leaving the country. A good deal for western investors — colonialism without the colonists.

Crippled by debts and high inflation, things worsened for Argentina throughout the 1990s. What all this adds up to is that Argentina has been on the receiving end of free-market 'shock therapy'. Heralded as the new winning formula for hard-up countries in the third world, through conditional loans and structural reforms, a heady mix of privatisation (sell all your nationalised industries), market liberalisation (float your currency and get rid of protective trade tariffs) and decreased public spending was forced on them.

This is where most crises start: strict adherence to what is called the 'Washington Consensus' the 'our way or the highway' approach enforced upon the majority of the poor world by hard-nosed Reganites, conditions on loans from the IMF, Wall Street financiers and the US treasury since the 1980s. The result was, and still is, the lining of pockets of western banks and investors which dealt a crushing blow for the majority of people in the developing world.

So, the 'Washington Consensus' was good medicine for Argentina right? Wrong. Rather than the expected windfall from the sale of these national assets, by 2000, unemployment had soared to over 30 per cent while the country's elite lined their foreign bank accounts to the tune of over $70 billion. Debt increased from around $8 billion in the late 1970s, to an unprecedented level of $150 billion by 2002. Over this same period, Argentina had paid $220 billion in interest. De La Rua, Menem's successor and President of the Alianza (a mix of the Radical and Frepaso parties) between 1999 and 2001, offered few new solutions and increased the pace of free market reforms. Unemployment, lack of food and unpaid wages continued to fuel discontent. From

July 2001, economic minister Cavallo introduced his 'zero deficit' policy which cut government employees' salaries and pensions and limited government spending which only increased the crisis. National strikes, road blocks and looting became daily occurrences in 2001. By this date, 50 per cent, nearly 20 million people, lived in a state of extreme poverty. The politics of hunger and misery were showing their full effect.

The downturns and crises rippling around the world economy in the Middle East, Mexico and Brazil were the last straw for Argentina. Smelling a home crisis, 'hot money' which had flowed quickly into Argentina, flowed out just as quickly due to the country's now open and liberalised financial sector. As foreign investors, the middle classes and the ruling elite shifted their money abroad, the government couldn't afford its public spending bill. Fulfilling its historic, heavy-handed role as it had done in Russia and East Asia previously, the IMF stepped in with a $40 billion bail-out loan in January 2001. This was to be the last IMF loan to Argentina before the country went into economic meltdown. But its harsh conditions further weakened domestic control of the economy and brought with them more deadly public spending cuts which sparked more poverty, food shortages and rioting. All these IMF loans do is prop up an over-valued currency for a now 'loan-addicted' govern-ment, offering it an easy way out of its problems. Worse still, while the IMF kept piling money into the economy to prop up the peso, wealthy Argentinians and international banks could make a fortune speculating on the over-valued currency.

DECEMBER 2001 INTERLUDE: ECONOMIC MELTDOWN, THE TEMPORARY DOWNFALL OF NEOLIBERALISM AND THE RISE OF PEOPLE POWER

My wife said to me, "crazy don't go out into the street anymore, they'll bring you back in a box. Think of your kids". But perhaps I'm not fighting for my kids. Of late, the alternative is to fight and die with dignity, or stay under the bed and die hungry like a rat.

THE MONTH OF DECEMBER 2001 didn't start well. On the 3rd, Cavallo ushered in the 'corralito' which meant bank withdrawals were limited to $250 a week. People were aghast as they saw their life savings frozen. Things moved from bad to worse. After the cosy ten year period of dollar parity, in January 2002, the peso was unpegged from the dollar and went into freefall. After rising to 5:1, it has now settled at a rate of about 3:1. So, if you had $100 pesos, before the crisis effectively you had $US100. However, now you would effectively only have $US33! Of course, the government saw that its big business friends didn't see their money disappear and bailed them out with public funds to cover their losses. There were also people in the know, who received

Left, "La libertad no es un show" (freedom is not a show) reads the grafitti scrawled on one of Buenos Aires' many monuments to the rich and powerful

Right, Thousands of people have gathered on the streets of Argentina's cities to bang their carcerolas (pots) and join in the carcerolazo — the way in which the people have made themselves heard to counter the 'deafness' of the ruling elite

advice or were shrewd enough to see the crisis coming and withdrew their money before the corralito. Many middle class families have saved their high consumption lifestyles by moving their life savings (in dollars) from the bank to a shoe-box or two under the stairs! However, one positive off-shoot of the devaluation is that since most Argentinians cannot afford imported goods and raw materials as they cost three times as much, the country is focusing, out of necessity, on making goods locally.

The overnight devaluation virtually wiped out a whole social class. Understandably, one of the most hated men in Argentina is Cavallo, especially amongst the angry ranks of the *ahorristas* (the savers) who were seen trying to break into the banks in December 2001 to get at their savings. Times were good before the crisis, people told us. You received your wages in over-inflated pesos and generally life was affordable. A middle class flourished who journeyed abroad and enjoyed the trappings of western lifestyles.

December 2001 got worse. Strikes and carcerolazos happened almost daily, bringing together middle class and working class people, raising fears that a situation of ungovernability was brewing. Lootings, mainly of large supermarket chains, increased and spread to the capital by the 18th December. Small shops were not targeted but rather the large multinational supermarkets, where people refused to leave until food was handed over. Most received it. There were a reported 9,000 lootings in Greater Buenos Aires, affecting 20 per cent of supermarkets, with losses at the big chains amounting to $US30 million. Things came to a head on the 19th and 20th. De la Rua called a state of emergency on the evening of the 19th at 9.00pm to try and halt the widespread lootings and blockades around the country which were now spreading into the capital. All gatherings, opposition parties and newspapers were banned and a curfew introduced.

The Government it seems chose unwisely. Few were going to accept a slide back into the old repressive days of military rule and what followed was the essence of the popular uprising. Despite the violent repression they'd suffered previously, the middle classes didn't stay inside but took to the streets with the unemployed, the piqueteros and the looters. 100,000 took to streets of Buenos Aires on the evening of the 19th. The diversity of people, young and old, unemployed, middle class, was remarkable. Massive police repression ensued. At 1.00am Cavallo resigned, but as morning broke and throughout the afternoon of the 20th, battles were fought on the streets of the capital. As mounted police troops rode through the city, people threw water and knives at them from balcony windows. 'It was like fighting a war in enemy territory', one person said from the San Telmo district of the capital. De la Rua resigned at 8.00pm later that day and fled in a helicopter. Over three days, there had been 35 dead, 439 injured, 3,200 arrested and one government defeated. In the next two weeks Argentina experienced four presidents ending with Eduardo Duhalde, former governor of Buenos Aires, being sworn in as President in January 2002.

Street battles in central Buenos Aires
Thousands take to the streets in spite of brutal police repression

The Notorious Bond
As the money ran out in many provinces, huge quantities of government bonds were printed to fill the vacuum

2001 REPRESENTED ONE OF THOSE MOMENTS of revolutionary excitement, a high point which brought together different groups through desperation and poverty under a common cause to oust the present

system and get involved in radical social change and self management. For those of us looking for evidence that people really can manage things themselves, it will go down in history, and no doubt be romanticised.

Yet the crisis of 2001 in Argentina, like nearly all other crises, was unable to break out of the usual cycle of: crisis, uprising, state repression, retreat, economic recovery and status quo (with on-going resistance against hunger and oppression). So, after a period where social unity, collectivism and solidarity went from strength to strength in 2002, by 2003 the inevitable stabilising of the economic crisis, the offer of jobs, the regaining of control by the unions and the streets by the police, meant that the demand, desire and energy for radical social change has been whittled back to the dedicated struggling for survival and the active struggling out of indignation.

So, 'people-led autonomy' has been weakened by the usual stuff — the recovery of the capitalist economy and corporate activity, an increase in prosperity and normalisation of middle class life, the desire for stability away from the spectre of renewed crisis, complacency and a return to individualism rather than collectivism, increasing state oppression led by the police and other more difficult to control paramilitary forces, and the return of the usual fears, divisions and stereotypings between social groups largely fuelled by the media. As a result, the initial backing offered by the middle/ upper classes had largely been withdrawn as their fears of crisis have subsided and normality has partially returned. For those with more immediate needs, the latest plan brought in to alleviate poverty amongst the unemployed is the *Plan de Jefes y Jefas* (limited social benefits of $150 pesos per month for the heads of households) which was a recommend-ation by the IMF to stop the crisis bubbling over. The problem is how to maintain the momentum of the uprising through the long haul. On the bright side,

we saw many examples of this collective spirit for radical change living on. When the next crisis comes, there will only be more people on the streets.

Economic life is far from normal. Many businesses still face bankruptcy. Take a trip around Buenos Aires today and you still see the same high-priced imported goods like furniture, cars and clothes. But now they are three times more expensive than they were before 2001 and well out of the price range for the majority of Argentinians. Mortgages and loans too are still repayable in dollars while people only have the weaker peso to make repayments. Normal goods like mate (the nation's drink) and coffee are more expensive too. To the disgust of the wealthy *porteños*, armies of *cartoneros* (people who collect cardboard to sell it) make their daily rounds through people's rubbish to collect this valuable resource. In 2001 they received 80 cents a kilo, but now even the cartoneros can't make a living as cardboard is worth only 23 cents per kilo.

In the wake of the economic crisis of 2001, people are also stuck with an unpopular government invention — the bond. There are $7.5 billion pesos of these circulating. These were crisis alleviation measures by the government to increase the circulation of 'money' and pay wages where there was little hard currency. Hence, the 'Patacon' was introduced in the Province of Buenos Aires and the 'Lecop' was introduced across the rest of the country. Other provinces introduced their own bonds tied to the local area. Try spending these outside the place of issue and you'll be met with a straight no and some worthless bits of paper in your pocket. While the bonds have helped money circulate where there were money shortages, given workers unpaid wages and ways to pay bills, and have stopped many people going hungry, many places won't accept them (especially if you want anything imported) and in many places you won't receive their face value. Most bonds have an expiry date of 2006 when the government promises to pay 135 per cent of the face

Fortress Banks
Most banks in downtown Buenos Aires are enclosed by protective metal walls used to keep out the hordes of people demanding their money. Almost without exception, the walls are daubed with grafitti expressing hatred of the banks

value of the bond! However, the majority of people we talked to were eager to get rid of these bits of paper and exchange them for hard cash. Graffiti on the bank of Boston in downtown Buenos Aires which reads 'Government thieves, gives us our money not bonds' just about sums it up. A local alternative to the capitalist money economy this isn't.

At face value, politically things are looking up in Argentina. In May 2003, the relatively unknown Nestor Kirchner was chosen as the new president of Argentina in a bizarre set of circumstances after Carlos Menem won the first round of voting and then stood down. With a tiny popular mandate, around 20 per cent of the total vote, Kirchner had to go to great lengths to win popular support. And he did fairly well. He stood up to the IMF and forced a cleansing of the army, the supreme court and the police. The Spanish judge Garzon now wants to extradite and try the infamous Ricardo Cavallo, nicknamed 'el serpico' who was hiding under a different name in Mexico for several years and was previously head of the notorious Navy Mechanics School where he was responsible for 264 disappearances and 159 kidnappings, including 16 pregnant women. Julio Nazarem, head of the supreme court, also resigned in June 2003 who represented one of the pillars of Menem's regime and gave impunity to many murderers from the dirty war. Military leaders are also voicing their disquiet as they face 47 cases for extradition. Kirchner has also distanced himself from the neoliberal excesses of his Peronist predecessor Menem. He has made it more difficult for foreign firms to pull out of the country and has put new conditions on inward investment. Since defaulting on its loans in September 2003, becoming the IMF's biggest debtor, Kirchner has refused to have conditions imposed upon them which would bring more misery. Yet there is little Kirchner can do while the country is straddled with such huge debts and IMF-imposed public spending cuts. Whether he can achieve anything more radical within the confines of the Peronist party is also highly debatable.

GOING HORIZONTAL
BEING AUTONOMOUS

ARGENTINA REPRESENTS AN UNFORGETTABLE popular revolutionary moment for lots of reasons. Images of thousands of people saying 'enough' and using their power to depose a president is for us in the comfortable West, a remarkable, and unsettling, sight. Behind this popular power was, if only temporarily, some real unity which brought together many different groups and individuals. A common shout on many demos still remains:

Piquete, carcelazo! La lucha es una sola!
(The struggle is one)

Many people involved in the popular uprising believe that the solution is to 'get rid of them all' (the bosses and politicians), and in their place have 'a government made up of neighbourhood assemblies and piqueteros'. A desire to do politics differently, to get rid of the legacy of corrupt bosses, politicians and military leaders is at the heart of the current spirit of Argentina. What sums it up for us is a desire to help yourself, and each other — to organise horizontally, without leaders and with respect, dignity and purpose. People are taking back control and setting up their own economy ranging from squatted allotments to temporary street kitchens.

The popular uprising contains an unbelievable variety of people. One of the things you notice is how groups organise. For example, some groups cling to old style 'vertical' structures such as the traditional leftist groups peddling trotskyist ideas and organising in fairly predictable command and control ways — voting, directing their members and controlling

Huerta Comunitaria
Community gardens are springing up all over the place, like this one on squatted land in the La Boca district of Buenos Aires

Community kitchen
These makeshift kitchens pepper the landscape, providing free food for anyone who needs it

*Top right, ronda de
pensamiento*
Roundtable discussions are a
common feature of grassroots
groups; ideas, actions and
theories are all thrashed out
collectively

Lower right, COPA
The aim of COPA is that everyone
is heard and has their say

and limiting energy and creativity out on the streets.
But more often, you come across those who are
committed to developing horizontal methods of
organising — using consensus decision making and
using small working and affinity groups without
leaders. Roundtable events, called *mesas* or *rondas*,
are popular ways of discussing issues, where everyone
has an equal say and chair persons are replaced by
voluntary facilitators or free-flowing discussions.
Committees are replaced by networks which bring
together groups who share common beliefs that they
can organise locally and for themselves.

Why has there been this move? Early on,
most groups have come realise that using
committees, leaders and delegating authority just
replicates old problems that got them into this mess
in the first place. The old ways of organising are
used by the government, trade unions, big firms and
the military and since it is these who are identified
as the source of misery for most Argentinians, then
new styles are needed. A key phrase used by groups
is that they are looking to be independent or
autonomous, or at least self-reliant, linking up in
loose networks with like-minded groups across the
country, but without any central command to control
their activities. They also want to be popular —
which means engaging the desires of the people
rather than a small governing elite.

TO THE STREETS!
PIQUETERO, CARAJO!

*You have to construct a new society every day: at the
picket, at the march, at the union, in the family, with
your friends, with music, with dance, with culture.
For these reasons, the picket is more than where it
happens. It's a culture. Pickets lack baths and water,
but there is happiness of the shared struggle, there's
plenty of soup for everyone, there's solidarity, there's
a different society.*

PIQUETEROS ARE GROUPS OF PEOPLE who block
roads, the piquete (the picket) is their weapon. With no
workplace left in which to demonstrate, unemployed
workers have blocked roads to demand food, money
and work. Denied the 'strike' as an organising tool,
they have resorted to other ways of disrupting the
economy like preventing the circulation of goods and
the functioning of the transport network. But as we
can see from the above quote, it is much more than
this. Road blocks have become a regular feature of
the Argentinian crisis since 1997 when in that year
there were 140. By 2002, there were nearly 2,000.
By coming together in this way, piqueteros have
realised that their demands are much greater —
not just work, but a new type of society. Piquetes are
also about regaining control of your demands and
the right to protest publicly and in the street, and not

ONE OF THE STRENGTHS OF THE AUTONOMOUS MOVEMENT IN ARGENTINA IS THE DESIRE TO BUILD A NETWORK OF HORIZONTAL GROUPS. ONE OF THE MAIN EXAMPLES IS COPA — THE COORDINATOR OF POPULAR AUTONOMOUS ORGANISATIONS (COORDINADORA DE ORGANIZACIONES POPULARES AUTÓNOMAS). SINCE ITS FOUNDING IN SEPTEMBER 2001, ITS AIMS HAVE BEEN TO PROMOTE POLITICS AND A SOCIETY BASED UPON AUTONOMY, DIRECT DEMOCRACY, POPULAR SOLIDARITY AND CONFRONTATIONS WITH THE CAPITALIST SYSTEM THAT THEY BELIEVE CONDEMNS PEOPLE TO HUNGER AND MISERY. COPA INCLUDES UNEMPLOYED WORKERS, FARMERS, STUDENT GROUPS AND SEVERAL POLITICAL, CULTURAL AND NEIGHBOURHOOD ASSEMBLY GROUPS. IT BELIEVES IN THE CONSTRUCTION OF POPULAR POWER IN WHICH THE PEOPLE BECOME SOCIAL AND POLITICAL ACITIVISTS THROUGH STRUGGLING FOR A DIFFERENT SOCIETY, BUILDING THEIR ORGANISATIONS AND MAKING LINKS WITH OTHERS. THEY REJECT THE IDEA OF VANGUARDS AND LEADERS OR THE IDEA THAT THEY THEMSELVES CARRY THE TRUTH, BUT INSTEAD SEE THE NEED TO DEVELOP PRACTICAL RESPONSES APPROPRIATE FOR EACH PLACE. COPA HAS ORGANISED FOUR NATIONAL ASSEMBLIES SINCE SEPTEMBER 2001 IN LA PLATA, SOLANO, ROSARIO AND QUIMILÍ.

relying on the anonymous hierarchy and bureaucracy of trade unions for change. The miners' strike of 1984–85 in the UK shared similar levels of militancy, disruption, solidarity and police brutality with the piqueteros of Argentina. During the strike, pickets became a part of daily life and a key tactic in the battle against the state. But what was different in the UK was the all encompassing control of the National Union of Mineworkers (NUM), and the absence of successful, occupations or the emergence of autonomous workers movements after the strike.

Argentina has a long tradition of working class solidarity and organising in the face of poverty, unemployment and corrupt politics. Piqueteros are part of working class struggles in Argentina dating back over one hundred years which brought together anarchists and socialists. The modern day piquetero movement was born during the privatisations of the 1990s. Argentina's state monopolised oil industry, YPF (Yacimientos Petrolificos Argentinos), was privatised in 1991. When this struggling and inefficient oil giant moved to the private hands of Spain's Repsol, there followed widespread closures, mainly due to pressures from US shareholders. It was in the wake of this that the piquetero movement was born in the large oil producing regions on the poor rural fringes like General Mosconi, Neuquén, and Cutral Co. Many communities dependent on the oil industry were devastated overnight. Prior to privatisation, over 51,000 people worked in the oil industry, the number now is around 5,000. Repsol YPF is now claimed to make profits of $2,400 every minute. What this amounts to, according to one trade union, is that 27 of the working days of the month generate pure profit for the company while the workers wages are paid in the other three days.

Communities here started to organise themselves against closures by creating movements of unemployed workers and blocking roads to demand work, benefits and food. The piqueteros gained wide support from civil society and so don't just include unemployed people, but people from all sections of society. There was a sense of a common cause, and that they could be next.

Within the piquetero movement there are many differences. One way to understand it is the difference between suave (soft) or duro (hard) piqueteros, which mainly reflects how many links they have with the government. The suaves, are often seen to have sold out as they negotiate with the state, or offer alternative routes when blocking roads. Links between piqueteros and the state are not surprising considering the historic links between heavy industry and official, often Peronist, trade unions. Much activity is organised through the large Peronist unions like the Central of Argentinian Workers (CTA), the General Confederation of Labour (CGT) or the Land, Life and Shelter Federation (FTV). As a result, many of these types of piquetero groups are based around prominent union leaders, work hierarchically, often bowing to government pressure, and are accused of manipulation of workers. In some cases, their leaders receive money from the rank and file members. The duros in contrast, also called the fogoneros (the burners), take the hardest line and refuse to talk to the government and continue more hardline direct action tactics of road blocking. Clearly there are many shades of grey in between, and most piquetes do bring together workers and citizens from all backgrounds who have realised their common struggle and show a strong desire to work together.

Numerous factions exist within the piquetero movement reflecting differences of tactics and ideology. The Bloque Piquetero (BP) established in 2002 is one of the most prominent and is itself made up of the Polo Obrero, Co-ordinadora de Unidad Barrial

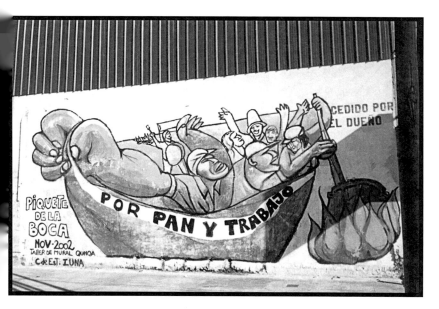

PIQUETE DE LA BOCA
NOV·2002
TALLER DE MURAL QUHOA
C·R·E·i·T. I.UNA

POR PAN Y TRABAJO

CEDIDO POR EL DUEÑO

For bread and work
A depiction of the road blocks in the La Boca district of Buenos Aires

the FTV and have become distanced from the above groups. In particular, the decision by the CCC-CTV-FTV to negotiate with the government has cut them off from BP and the MTDs. In many ways, these differences have weakened the movement and the piquetero struggle, but for others they have strengthened the resolve to stay committed to the ideology of confrontation to achieve their demands.

(CUBA), Federación de Trabajadores Combativos (FTC), Movimiento Territorial y Liberacion (MTL) and the Movimiento Teresa Rodriguez (MTR). The BP often joins with the MTD Anibal Veron and other groups such as MIJD and Barrios de Pie who collectively take a more confrontational stance and stay committed to road blocks. Other piquetero groups are linked more to the Peronist trade unions like the Maoist Corriente Clasista Combativa (CCC), the Central de Trabajadores Argentinos (CTA) and

1996 saw the first National Meeting of Unemployed Workers in the province of Neuquén. It was in this same province, in the town of Cutral Co that some of the most organised road blocks emerged in 1997 in response to gas and electricity supplies being cut. A year later saw the first march in Buenos Aires organised against hunger, unemployment and repression. Throughout this time, piquetero groups were involved in road blocks, regional and national strikes while also holding discussions with the government demanding larger unemployment benefits. In 1999 when the Alliance came to power, relations between the government and the piquteros worsened. Social spending was cut, the government voted on the flexibilisation of labour, and the government used force against the rising number of road blocks, which had now started in the national capital. The new president De la Rua and his Minister of the Interior, Storani, set out to defeat the piqueteros on a national scale. In June 2001, the Government waged a particularly bloody battle against the unemployed oil workers of General Mosconi in the province of Salta.

In July 2001, the first National Assembly of Piqueteros was held which voted on a series of national strikes, and demanded the release of prisoners and an increase in benefits to $380 pesos per family. It brought together groups from the whole country, and this diversity gave it a truly revolutionary feeling. In early December piquetero groups — CTA and Frenapo — undertook a Popular Consultation in which nearly three million people expressed their opinions in relation to increasing benefits for unemployed people. During the clashes of 19th and 20th December, the difference between how the government treated the piqueteros and other more middle class groups like those involved in the carcelerazos, couldn't be more stark. The incoming President Duhalde continued the commitment to defeat the piquetero movement through a number of bloody attacks on those blocking roads, which left two dead in Buenos Aires on June 26th 2002. The piqueteros and unions have

been an important part in keeping up the pressure. The CTA union, for example, called a general strike on 29th May 2002 which involved road blocks throughout the country.

One of the main functions of the piquetero groups is to distribute government unemployment benefits to its members. By 2002, the Piquetero Block contained 35,000 people and distributed 20,000 benefits per month which were worth $150 pesos per week. Unemployment benefits have been a key resource for unemployed groups in their efforts for self-management. The government has tried to stem the growth of independent workers and piquetero groups by setting up NGOs and using local elites controlled by Peronist parties and unions to distribute unemployment plans. But the piquetero groups have retaliated by setting up their own NGOs to collect these plans, to coordinate actions, self organise and maintain their autonomy. However, out of the nearly two million unemployment plans distributed by the government in 2002, only 128,000 were distributed by piqutero groups. Horizontal piquetero groups remain committed to self-management of government funds as they see this as the most effective way of meeting local needs. While such dependency on government hand-outs undermines their autonomy, these funds are an essential part of survival for the millions of unemployed Argentinians. Channelled through the MTDs, it is also money with few strings attached which can be used for setting up autonomous projects such as bakeries and brick workshops.

THE MOVEMENT OF UNEMPLOYED WORKERS (MTDS) 'FOR WORK, DIGNITY AND SOCIAL CHANGE'

"The organisation of the MTDs is horizontal... the deliberations and the decision are taken in assemblies open to the neighbourhood. A flat organisation and the continuous exercise of participation constitutes one of the defining characteristics of these movements. We are brought up with two big lies: one is to do with religion — when you die you're going to be okay The other: when we have a revolution everyone is going to be happy. We don't have to wait until the revolution to be happy — to start to construct a new person. We start to construct the new person today. From our political vision, autonomy can't exist if it's not collective. And this collective autonomy implies responsibilities, for everyone and between everyone. Responsibility to construct, to promise, to respect your friends to love each other every day."

THESE WORDS FROM ONE MEMBER OF THE MTD movement (in Castilian, *El Movimiento de Trabajadores Desocupados*) show their commitment a new way of doing politics. Their logo combines the desire for meaningful work but also the need for change: 'For work, dignity and social change'. The MTDs are basically groups of unemployed people who have come together in their neighbourhoods to provide services, make food, provide shelter, sell their products, educate themselves, and get involved collectively in demonstrations. The strength of the MTDs has been in their creation of a parallel economy, funded by the unemployment benefits they receive, based on meeting community needs. Three areas which have been particularly developed are the panaderia, the bloquera and the ropero — the bakery, block making workshops and clothes shop.

Left, Las abuelas tejiendo
Mothers and grandmothers from MTD Solano crocheting hats in the main square of Buenos Aires during a demonstration against the Government. Not a minute is wasted during the solidarity economy!

Right, ¡Piquete carajo!
Memebers of the MTD take part in blocking one of the major roads into Buenos Aires on the 26th June 2003

Everything which the MTD does is geared towards disengagement with the formal economy and the creation of a local, independent 'economia solidaridad' — the solidarity economy. There is work for everyone, and all of it is valued highly. The *abuelas tejiendo* (the crocheting grannies) for example, make hats for everyone for the long, cold Argentinian winters. In essence, the autonomous workers movement is attempting to reorganise the culture of work — to make it meaningful and linked to local needs. So, horizontal organising is one of the key aims of the future politics put forward by the MTDs. However, there are barriers to this since many of the unemployed workers coming to the MTDs come from large factories steeped in more hierarchical and Peronist-based union based ways of organising. Still, with time, most compañeros in the MTDs have realised that self-management has allowed them to meet their own and their community's needs in a fuller and dignified way.

MTDs are mostly neighbourhood-based, and many people come from the same former workplaces. The power base of the MTDs is in the poorer areas of the province of Buenos Aires and the provinces of Argentina. The MTDs emerged in the mid-to-late 1990s in response to the needs of unemployed groups. The first were formed in the poor neighbourhoods of Buenos Aires in Varela and Solano. They are keen to stress their horizontalness — that is collective decision making, no leaders, and no connections with political parties. Many people in Argentina today look to the MTDs as an example of organising community work and community relations beyond the money economy. The MTDs have been at the centre of the piquetero movement and the fight for survival of unemployed Argentinians. They represent some of the most dedicated, confrontational and uncompromising piqueteros, refusing to negotiate or concede to government demands or sweeteners.

The MTDs have grown into a prominent national organisation and in 2001 the Coordinator of Unemployed Workers of Anibal Veron (CTDAV) was formed to coordinate the more horizontal MTDs throughout the country, although there are still MTDs outside this structure. Anibal Veron was a chauffer for the Atahualpa company, in Mosconi, Salta. In the repression of 2001 he was killed by the police during a picket whilst trying to claim the three months of pay owed to him by the company. Amongst the MTDs of Anibal Veron, there are three in the province of Rio Negro (in the north of Argentina), and the rest are within the province and federal district of Buenos Aires. These include:

MTD Solano
MTD Lanús
MTD Darío Santillán de Almirante Brown
MTD Florencio Varela
MTD Guernica
MTD Quilmes
MTD Esteban Echeverría
MTD Oscar Barrios de José C. Paz
MTD Berisso
MTD La Plata
MTD Lugano
MTD San Telmo
MTD Parque Patricios
MTD 26 de junio de La Matanza
MTD 23 de Julio

By the middle of 2002, CTDAV had 15,000 members and had distributed 9,000 unemployment benefits per month. Solano remains one of the largest MTDs, made up of seven neighbourhoods and with its own health commission and orchard. Interestingly in 2003, MTD Solano took the decision to withdraw from Anibal Veron as they said it was restricting their autonomy.

The 'Movement Teressa Rodriguez' is another prominent piquetero group who broke away from the MTD in 1997. Teressa was a teacher who was forced to work as a cleaner and who was killed in 1997 in road blocks in Cutral Co. The ideology of MTR is summed up by one member: "we have our own production projects, we don't need any municipality or state, nor the thieves or assassins, to tell us what to do". However, MTR does use more vertical and traditional organising structures, with clear lines of responsibility between organisers and members.

Merendero in San Telmo
In the busy offices of MTD San Telmo, members organise an after-school kids club, while others prepare the evening meal or arrange products for sale in the shop

28TH JUNE 2003
TAKING CONTROL IN
THE NEIGHBOURHOOD
MTD SAN TELMO

MTD SAN TELMO IS TUCKED AWAY under the southern approach motorway which, lifted on stilts, rips Buneos Aires apart on its south side. It is a small, humble building, not the most aesthetically pleasing with its rusty window grills and splintered glass. However, the constant life makes up for the urban decay. As we approached one afternoon to visit, the *merendero* (children's tea time activities) was in full swing. A throng of children swarmed outside the door, running in and out of the building, jumping up and down on the back of an open-backed truck. Unprompted, the children started to shout 'cabrones, ladrones!' (bastards, thieves). Not directed at us we hoped, as we stood there, slightly out of place as the only gringos on the street, looking at them. Then the real source of discontent was revealed as two policemen slowly walked past, the children ecstatic in their insults, the police threatening in the glares and the adults of MTD quietly ecstatic trying to conceal their laughter and pride at the well executed and well learnt insults from the kids towards the state.

Inside, the building consisted of a large room fitted out with a kitchen and oven at the back and tables at the front doubling as a meeting, eating and social space. Cabinets on the wall to one side and in the window displayed products which the unemployed workers of San Telmo made for sale: washing detergent, fruit liquors, jams, mate pots, hats and gloves. Over an obligatory mate, a few of the members who were preparing dinner told us a bit about how they organise. There were two main types of groups — community ones and productive ones — which according to a sheet of paper on the wall where people signed up for tasks, were divided up as follows:

Community groups
School help
Merendero (activities for kids)
Communal kitchen
Bread making
Maintenance
Fairs (selling products)

Production groups
Sewing
Sweets/jams
Cleaning
Liquors
Materia (mate)

The members told us that they were very definitely a 'horizontal' group. Decision making was done collectively at the weekly meetings and being a member entailed numerous responsibilities. These were set out on another piece of paper on the wall:

* Everyone participates in the groups Monday to Friday

* Everyone has to come to the weekly assembly to participate

* If you don't attend for three days, you have to reapply to the group

* Everyone has to pay $1 peso per week to cover food costs

* Everyone has to participate in demonstrations

* No alcohol allowed in the building

This wasn't just a mere list on the wall. We saw the compañeros of MTD San Telmo fulfilling these duties on many occasions — eating together, caring for each others kids, making bread and things to sell, and demonstrating on the streets for their rights and for work.

Could you tell us about the history of MTD Solano?

In 1997, August more or less, a group of neighbours who had been tolerating the shady management of government benefits for the unemployed got tired of the way things were being done. One of the things had been that to join benefit programs people had to pay money to local PJ groups [The PJ is the ruling Peronist party in Argentina who have been the main political party since the 1950s under the popular dictator General Juan Peron], so the neighbours started to meet to struggle together against unemployment. A local church was the only place that opened its doors to us, partly because some of the group used to work in the church.

The 8th August was our first meeting, then we had various assemblies, we were defining ourselves, not as a political party or a trade union organization but on the experience of other compañeros for example, Cutral Co in the south, Tartagal in the north, Varela here, so we decided to be a Movimento de Trabajadores Desocupados. It began as a faithful copy of the compañeros of Varela, with a vertical structure and a general secretary. Then in various assemblies as an MTD we discussed what should be our slogans and we made the slogan of our struggle — work, dignity and social change.

From this we started to go from place to place building our movement, our first road block was done with the compañeros from Varela. They cut Route 36 to get social benefits and we went with them to help in this blockade. Then in November we did a coordinated action. Through lack of experience and organization in planning this type of protest and because we were new, the blockade lasted a week and ended with the arrest of 28 compañeros.

This all caught the attention of the Bishop of the diocese of Quilmes and he warned the priest that things like this shouldn't be happening in their area whilst the diocese received a subsidy from the province for maintenance of the canteens, nurseries and schools of $3,000 a month. At this point Duhalde was the governor of the province. Therefore the Bishop transferred the priest to another area. We were against this act and realized that no organization could develop fully under the protection of the church. This generated a conflict culminating in the occupation of the church for two years and in the middle of a discussion with the province, municipality and bishop they evicted us using arms in June 2000. We were violently interrupted whilst groups of compañeros were cooking. There were families living there because we had converted the space into a hostel for homeless people. They were treated violently in their home by the police.

After that episode we moved to our present location [an area of reclaimed land] and coordinated with other movements doing massive road blockades, with three or four organisations and a eal growth of the movement started. In November 2001, there were 350 people in the assembly and 150 with benefits — all resulting from the blockades. Then the community leaders saw that it was starting to become dangerous, we proposed in the workshops the right to work with more dignity, thereby reclaiming work clothes, shoes and tools by means of the strikes in the workshops. Finally, we succeeded that 'women's day' and the 'day of the sick' were respected and this generated a new conflict with the community leaders. So in 1998, the leaders started to pressurise us to abandon the MTD, threatening us with the loss of their benefits, so lots of compañeros left and numbers decreased to 30.

From this grew the idea of autonomy. In 2001, we were still with the MTD and we'd grown again to 800 and we put ourselves forward with the principles of autonomy, horizontality, direct democracy and struggle. We decided to use the benefits as a means rather than an end and started to develop workshops and mini ventures where we could eventually self-sustain ourselves, a concept which we are still discussing within the movement — an organisation of work without exploitation and where every one would be the owner of their tools. Today there are bakeries and community gardens which aim at self sufficiency and think about the dignity of feeding ourselves without genetically modified food. To make healthy food and the protein our bodies need to develop. The garden workshops happen in almost every neighbourhood, there is also a more ambitious project in an abandoned factory we have that was given to us by the Mothers of Plaza de Mayo, there we want to develop an organic garden and a farm to breed rabbits and chickens. The project aims to use the meat of the rabbits for the canteens and the skin for other uses, the chickens will also be used this way, whilst the garden should produce a bank of organic seeds.

In these six years, we have seen that within popular organizations it is very difficult to organise and coordinate. Today, this coordination exists thanks to the efforts that the people of Varela made respecting different political affiliations. We are against and we fight whichever system of domination exists, call it what you call it, it has to do with dignity. We are convinced that we are capable to choose rather than accept.

One of the forms in which we implemented horizontality, apart from getting rid of the post of secretary was to create work areas, so within the movement several areas exist — health, administration, press, relations with organisations and visits, finance — which is the work area which looks at the spending of the movement through a common fund. They don't control it, more oversee it. There is another work area which is planning which establishes what to do with regard to the needs put forward by the members. In the seven geographical areas where the movement exists there are these work areas. With respect to the area of health, when this was created we also built a pharmacy, a people's pharmacy, which cost about 1,300 Argentinian pesos. In each area there are assemblies where the activities of the movement are discussed, they discuss who will enter each work area. These assemblies lead to a general meeting of the areas with delegates from each work area who bring plans, worries, doubts and conflicts that arise in each area, the delegates then take back information to their area to rediscuss the issues and finally come back to a general meeting to make final decisions. This fortifies and consolidates the participation of the compañeros in decision making, maybe it doesn't go deep enough into some subjects. Where there is deeper discussion is in the training workshops in which compañeros use popular education techniques.

Did you vote in the recent elections?

We called for people not to vote, but equally we respected those compañeros who choose to vote, but the autonomous movement put forward a call NOT TO VOTE, we analysed the candidates, but only in terms of knowing our enemy. With respect to religion it is the same, the movement has no chosen religion.

How many people are there in Solano MTD?

In total, almost 500 within seven neighbourhoods. On a national level there are 7,000 in the MTD, with 17 movements throughout the country.

Is Solano the biggest?

Before we were one of the biggest with 1,500 members, but now we are one of the smaller ones, I don't know which is biggest.

What is this area like and what are the problems here?

At the start the zone was populated through the appropriation of fiscal lands by people from the north of the province, then came foreigners from bordering countries, mainly Paraguay and Bolivia. It is an industrial manufacturing zone, but after 1994 the big factories declined and disappeared, generating a lot of unemployment and high levels of pollution due to the large amount of factories that there were.

Of these, the factories that caused the most pollution were the tanneries and they caused lead contamination. There is still a cellulose factory that causes a lot of pollution. Another problem related to the pollution of aquifers due to the privatisation of water. These are the forgotten neighbourhoods, neighbourhoods with unpaved roads, with few transports services, of great precariousness.

What are the challenges you face in the future?

Unemployment is something that has motivated us to organise, the objective is to one day have a more dignified life, we won't find real work within the capitalist system, we have to create our own sources of work, without oppression or domination. Everything that comes from the system is because it suits the system, Kirchner is one more from within the system and up to now he hasn't done anything to improve the situation for those within the autonomous movements. For us governments are those we are struggling against.

Interview available in Spanish at: *http://www.geog.leeds.ac.uk/publications/city/*

26TH JUNE 2003
NOT EVEN IN DEATH,
WILL THEY STOP US! (¡NI
MUERTOS, NOS DETENDRAN!)
THE ANNIVERSARY OF THE
MASSACRE OF AVELLANEDA
BUENOS AIRES

ON 26TH JUNE 2002, DARIO SANTILLAN AND MAXI Kosteki were murdered by the Argentinian police. They were amongst the 4,000 other piqueteros — the unemployed workers of Argentina — who blocked and demonstrated on the Pueyrredon Bridge in Avellaneda on the southern edge of Buenos Aires demanding food and work, and an end to political corruption. Around midday, over 400 armed police officers advanced in two columns towards the bridge. What exactly happened next is still subject to much debate. However, Maxi was shot and mortally wounded as he ran for cover towards a nearby train station, where shortly after he died. Dario was determined to stay with his dying friend, one hand grasping Maxi´s, the other outstretched towards the police who aimed at him. Ordered to leave, as Dario ran towards the exit, he was shot.

A year later, 26th June 2003. 40,000 people gather on the bridge at Avellaneda for the anniversary of the massacre and again block the major arterial route into the city. Maxi, 23 years old,

and Dario, 21 years old, both piqueteros with the *Movimiento de Trabajadores Desocupados Anibal Veron*, were some of the first victims of the new Argentinian regime after the popular rebellion of December 2001. Dario and Maxi, as they are affectionately known, were heros, brothers, friends, compañeros, workers. The demo was a show of strength and defiance of great importance in the face of ongoing state repression, impunity and an economic crisis which isn´t letting up for the unemployed, who number over a third of the population. A dizzying array of groups — piqueteros, desocupados, artists, students, community assemblies, independent media — were present on the anniversary. Amongst the piquetero groups were the *Coordinadora de Trabajabores Desocupados Anibal Veron, Movimiento Territorial Liberación (MTL), Movimiento Teresa Rodríguez (MTR), Polo Obrero, Coordinadora Unidad Barrial (CUBA), Movimiento sin Trabajo (MST), Frente Trabajadores Combativos (MTC), Movimiento Independiente de Jubilados y Desocupados (MIJD)*.

As the crisis and popular rebellion of December 2001 begins to fade into the past, the groups assembled for the anniversary are a reminder that they are as strong, determined and organised as ever to build a new social and economic reality outside the corruption of the Argentinian government, the crippling demands of the IMF, deep-seated military and police repression, and US-led imperialism. In tune with the style of the popular uprising in Argentina, the 40,000 assembled participated in a *juicio popular* (people´s court) to serve justice on those who killed Dario and Maxi.

Juicio popular
Thousands gather, including many from the Mothers of the Plaza de Mayo, to listen to testimonies from the events of the 26th June 2002, during the People's Court held on the main motorway flyover leading into Buenos Aires

Asesinos
A list of the police and politicians responsible for the death of Dario and Maxi, written on a wall in the San Telmo district of Buenos Aires

to tell their own story, MTD Lanus had also published a book called *Dario and Maxi: Piquetro Diginity*, giving in-depth analysis and eye witness accounts of what happened on the bridge that day and why, and the build up of police repression surrounding it.

Eyewitnesses described how a plan by the government and police had been orchestrated at Avellaneda to attempt to break the piqueteros in June 2002. At that time, President Duhalde had a crucial forthcoming meeting with the IMF.

Several eye witness accounts of the massacre were presented along with a statement denouncing the impunity of government and police officials and demanding work and justice. As cries of *¡piqueteros carajo!* (We are Piqueteros!), and *Dario y Maxi presente* (Dario and Maxi are with us) filled the air, one person shouted 'we don't want a ceasefire with yankie imperialism, the only justice is the people's justice'. The popular conclusions to this 40,000 strong open air trial were numerous — death, blood and jail were amongst the final demands. In an effort

The Fund was getting nervous about the $US150 billion Argentinian debt and there were rumours in Washington that he was running a weak government which lacked control of its social movements. Eager to oblige, Duhalde flexed the muscles of his police force to prove he could put an end to the tactic of 'cortes' (road blocks) by the piqueteros and crush their power. Hence the massacre — a useful and well-used political tool for propping up corrupt regimes. Further, according to the 90 injured who arrived at a nearby hospital, the hospital director

work programmes, a large majority remain unconvinced and continue building another world. A short walk from Buenos Aires' prosperous waterfront, office towers and luxury apartments, reveals a growing social experiment which continues to expand in which people are finding more ways to meet their own needs. On most blocks, and many street corners, community assemblies, community kitchens, Unemployed Workers Movements, occupied factories many including social centres, and squatted houses continue their activities, providing food and shelter for the most needy, making and selling goods ranging from jam and clothes, to candles and cleaning products, running classes for school kids, baking bread, growing vegetables and running health commissions.

At the same time a vast community printing infrastructure produces and disseminates pamphlets and books, many explaining the movements aims and offering advise on how to join in the popular, self-management revolution. The MTDs are playing a

ordered the doors locked, hence most were denied treatment and later intimidated by the police. Official government reports the following day, claimed only rubber bullets were used and any deaths were accidental. However the presence of photographers who took close up photos of the events helped identify particular police with the deaths.

While many people are being lulled by the relative stabilisation of the peso, and the valiant attempts by the incoming president Nestor Kirchner to clean the country's major institutions and provide

Maxi and Dario ¡presentes!
*Memorial mural on Puete
Puyrredon, Avellaneda depicting
the road block of the piqueteros*

Maxi and Dario ¡presentes!
*Dario and Maxi are, after their
deaths, still very much part of
the struggle, depicted here
holding the Argentinian flag*

moment of December 2001 in Argentina, there are now less people involved in the popular struggle. The ever risk-aversive middle classes have retreated to a comfortable distance, giving back their faith to politicians and the democratic system rather than self-management and people power. However, for well over half the country's population, many living in the 'Villas Miserias' (shanty towns) and impoverished and de-industrialised outer provinces of Buenos Aires, the daily struggle

key organising role in this, providing a focus for community social service provision and organising socially useful production. Here, autonomy and horizontal decision making are the flavour of the day, and one is reminded of the Zapatista autonomous communities in Mexico's southern state of Chiapas, which are organising and self-managing thousands of communities, schools, community clinics and commercial centres across five zones, outside of, and openly hostile to, Mexican capitalist society and government.

Clearly, after the peak of the revolutionary

continues — out of necessity. While they have their enemies in sights and they have the skills and the dedication to build a different world, they have to face the constant threat of police violence, renewed social stigmatisation, and deepening economic crisis from new IMF structural reforms.

Violent evictions also continue — the one during Easter 2002 at the Brukman textile factory, only the most visible amongst countless cases of intimidations, lockouts and forced removals. And impunity for the ruling elite continues as police responsible for deaths in 2002 walk free. Maxi and

voices are part of the growing thousands who are continuing the popular, autonomous revolution in this corner of Latin America. As graffiti and murals across the city dedicated to Dario and Maxi tell us — not even in death, will they stop us!

Dario have become martyrs, heros for the movement and their communities. Their images are painted defiantly on the underpass leading to the Pueyrredon Bridge. Unfortunately, there are likely to be others. On the 26th of every month, people continue to gather on the bridge to remember them. But more importantly to remind themselves why they are struggling, what they are up against and provide each other with inspiration and hope. In Dario and Maxi, the MTD has lost two brave, inspirational, dedicated workers and compañeros. However, the movement takes strength from the fact these two

ASAMBLEAS POPULARES (POPULAR ASSEMBLIES) POWER IN THE NEIGHBOURHOOD

Lo que el pueblo construye,
los poderosos no lo destruirán
(What the people create, the powerful can't destroy)

The Asambleas Populares emerged out of the crisis of December 2001, when people took to the streets to oust the President and voice their discontent about *el corralito*. Neighbours who had never talked to each other found themselves marching together to the central demonstrations, banging their pans, running from bullets and going home together. This happened spontaneously but once people began talking and acting together, and De La Rua (the president) fled, they decided to carry on working collectively through neighbourhood popular assemblies which they saw as closer to democracy than the existing political system.

Because of these origins, the Asambleas are more neighbourhood based, and involve a mixture of people, both middle and working class, who are keen to get involved in self-organising and management at a neighbourhood level. They have recreated the sense of community that is often lost in urban environments, given people involved a sense that their opinions count and that they can change things on both a local and national level. People in each neighbourhood started gathering regularly on a street corner or local park to discuss how they could work together and how they saw the future. Often there was an *olla popular* — a huge pan of food for all to share.

From here some groups went on to occupy spaces (ironically often the empty banks) to use as meeting places, community centres and homes. Typically the Asambleas will hold weekly discussions — the ronda popular — on community issues but also on topics such as the external debt, war and free trade, and will have an info space and perhaps computers, books and various workshops on yoga, self defence, languages and basic skills. Many also have community gardens, run after school kids clubs and adult education classes, put on social and cultural events, cook food collectively, and mobilise politically for themselves and in support of the piqueteros and reclaimed factories.

In Buenos Aires, inter-area asambleas were held, with representatives from each neighbourhood asamblea in Parque Centenario, and then provincial and national asambleas were organised. Two months after the 2001 uprising, the National 'Assembly of Assemblies' called for a 'Government of the asambleas populares, workers and piqueteros'. Their resolution stated:

ONE ASAMBLEA IN BUENOS AIRES, ALMAGRO, USES THE SIDE OF A BRANCH OF BANCO FRANCES FOR ITS MEETINGS, PAINTING A INFO BOARD ON THE BANK'S WALL AND HOLDING AN *OLLA POPULAR* ON THE STREET OUTSIDE. GATHERING AROUND A LARGE PAN ONE NIGHT, HELPING LOCAL RESIDENTS PREPARE THEIR FORTNIGHTLY OLLA POPULAR, WE ARE STRUCK BY THE AGE AND SOCIAL MIX OF THE PEOPLE CHOPPING UP VEGETABLES, CHATTING AND SHARING MATE. TALKING TO THEM, WE DISCOVER THAT TWO YEARS AGO MOST OF THEM HAD NEVER MET OR TALKED. NOW THEY ORGANISE, COOK AND DEMON-STRATE TOGETHER AND HAVE RECREATED A STRONG SENSE OF UNITY AND LOCAL COMMUNITY.

"We must take into our own hands the solving of the most pressing problems of the masses — jobs, health, education, housing — which means spreading and promoting [asambleas populares, piquetero organisa-tions and workers' asambleas] up and down the country as an alternative which belongs to the people."

After the 2001 crisis, there were over 200 asambleas in Buenos Aires alone. Most had widespread support with thousands in each. Yet, over the last two years, support has dwindled back to the most committed people. As the financial situation has improved for some they have stopped relying on community support to survive, while others have found that working together is hard at times and requires commitment. Direct democracy, as people told us in the asambleas, means taking your life into your own

hands. It is hard work and requires much self belief. Police oppression and an economic turn-up has also led to an increasing number of violent evictions of the asambleas. However, you can still encounter them every few blocks as you wander through the city.

ASAMBLEA POPULAR CID CAMPEADOR

One of the most prominent Asambleas Populares in Buenos Aires is Cid Campeador. Hanging from the ceiling as you enter its squatted space (previously a foreign bank, left empty during the economic crisis) is a battered, old pot with its bottom bashed out. This pot tells the story of how it all started. "It was there from the start" Coco tells us. "It was involved in the carcerolazos of December 2001 and then many more before dying a valiant death and becoming a memorial to the successes of the popular movement. Its there to remind us not to stop struggling".

Cid Campeador is a People's Assembly in the neighbourhood of Almagro, in west central Buenos Aires. They formed during the cacerolazos of December 2001 and continued to meet in a local park, organising communal food and going together to protest against the Government's handling of the financial crisis. The area and the Assembly have a mixture of income groups, some poor, some comfortable, as well as students and unemployed. In 2002, the group decided that rather than hold their discussions and activities in the street they would make use of a disused building. So they found an old bank, an incredible building with marble tiles and mirrored walls. It now hosts meetings, after school

Top, Asamblea Popular Cid Campeador
This asamblea has mafe its home in a disused three-storey bank, and is used constantly by the local community

Below, the Pot
Inside Cid Campeador hangs a well-beaten pot as a reminder to the many times members have taken it on demonstations and used it in the carcerolazos

VIERNES 25 de julio - 19 horas

VECINAS Y VECINOS:

La ASAMBLEA POPULAR CID CAMPEADOR, cumple un año de recuperación para el barrio de nuestra casa.

Como parte del programa de actividades culturales, festivas y políticas que realizaremos en nuestro mes aniversario, los invitamos a una serie de debates abiertos.

QUEREMOS COMPARTIR LAS INQUIETUDES QUE NOS SON COMUNES, Queremos PENSAR JUNTOS, y ACORDAR PROPUESTAS, para convertirlas en realidad con la participación de todas y todos.

* ¿COMO ASEGURAR DE VERDAD LA SEGURIDAD TODOS LOS VECINOS?
* ¿ES POSIBLE DISTRIBUIR LA RIQUEZA DE VERDAD?
* ¿QUE HACER CON LAS EMPRESAS QUE FUERON CORRUPTAMENTE PRIVATIZADAS Y PRETENDEN ALZAS DE TARIFAS?
* ¿QUE PASA CON LA DEUDA EXTERNA QUE HACE AÑOS EL JUEZ BALLESTEROS FALLO QUE ES ILEGAL E ILEGITIMA Y SIN EMBARGO SE SIGUE PAGANDO CON EL HAMBRE DEL PUEBLO?

Invitamos a un primer encuentro el **VIERNES 25 DE JULIO A LAS 19 HS. En la Casa de la Asamblea Popular Cid Campeador, Avda. Angel Gallardo 752.**

Mesa Debate sobre:
LOS MOVIMIENTOS SOCIALES y
LA NUEVA SITUACION POLITICA NACIONAL E INTERNACIONAL

Participan:
Magdalena Jitrik (Colectivo Taller Popular de Serigrafía)
Vilma Ripol (diputada Izquierda Unida)
María Eva Blota (Colectivo Intergaláctica)
Toty Flores (Movimiento de Trabajadores Desocupados - La Matanza)
Daniel Campione (revista Periferia)
Claudio Katz (Economistas de Izquierda)

PRESENTACION DE LA REVISTA **CUADERNOS DEL SUR**

ASAMBLEA POPULAR CID CAMPEADOR

---

clubs, adult education classes, yoga, the Indymedia office and regular benefit gigs.

The walls are covered in posters and information about various campaigns and demonstrations around Argentina — serving as a valuable information point but also as a constant reminder that the Assemblies are not alone in their struggle for autonomy and self-management. From the Mapuche land struggle in Patagonia, and the HIJOS campaign for retribution for those responsible for genocide, to MTDs and the occupied factories, they are an instant introduction to the breadth of Argentina's social movements struggling in so many different ways but with similar beliefs in autonomy and the possibility of another Argentina run by the people.

THE INDIGENOUS STRUGGLE FOR LAND AND RIGHTS
MOVIMIENTO CAMPESINO DE SANTIAGO DE ESTERO (MOCASE)

ARGENTINA'S INDIGENOUS GROUPS are not well known. Most were ruthlesly repressed and exterminated. Few remain in comparison to neighbouring Peru and Bolivia and the thriving Mayan, Nahua, Olmec and Zapotec cultures of Mexico. However, journey out of the Europeanised Federal District of Buenos Aires towards the Chilean, Paraguayan or Bolivian border, and the ethnic difference is still remarkable.

One indigenous group which we spent time with was the Movimiento Campesino de Santiago de Estero (the Farmers Movement of the province of

Squat anniversary
Cid Campeador celebrates a year occupying a bank by inviting neighbours to a roundtable debate on social movements and the new national/international political situation!

41

Santiago de Estero). Living in the poor, state of Santiago de Estero, over a days drive from the country's capital, the farmers of MOCASE are far away from the dramatic urban struggles of the piqueteros and popular assemblies of Buenos Aires. But they have managed to provide an inspirational focal point for many people struggling for autonomy. For years, the farmers of Santiago have attempted to eek out a living on poor marginal lands, in this province which seems far removed from the bustling wealthy Federal District. For many people, the benefits of a modern-day society have hardly arrived and people still lack the basic necessities of life such as land, water and decent food.

The seeds of inspiration for MOCASE were sown from the 1950s, when many farmers were pushed off their lands by multinational companies eager to exploit resources such as timber and grow cash crops such as cotton and soya. The UK firm Forestal played a key role in the deforestation of the area. The farmers of the province have always faced tough conditions. They have lived under the regime of Carlos Juarez, who with his family and cronies, has governed the province for four decades through political clientalism, tough autocratic social control and granting special rights to large firms. MOCASE came into being in 1990 when several farmers groups came together at a place called *Los Juries* and decided there was a need for a united regional group to coordinate actions. Farming leaders of the time such as Ramon Gomez saw the need to disseminate information to educate other farmers of their rights to stop land evictions. Education about

land rights was based around raising awareness of the *Ley Veinteañal* (the 20 year law) that states that if you work the land for more than 20 years you become the deed holder. However, many firms were exploiting the farmers' ignorance of the law and evicting them from their lands, with the backing of

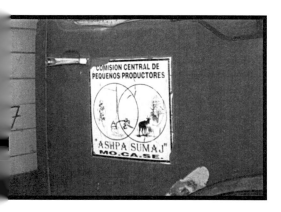

the provincial governor, and without compensation. In this way, MOCASE has empowered hundreds of small family producers to organise for themselves and stand up for themselves.

Today 8,000 families form MOCASE, with 58 communities spread over seven *centrales* or centres. These places are literally liberated zones, where members of MOCASE are experimenting and building for themselves. MOCASE works relatively horizontally with elected rotating delegates coming to each centre to represent their community every fifteen days. Most people in the communities have *cargos* (roles) which rotate every two years. In 1999, over 500 delegates attended their first congress. Over the 1990s, the groups have developed links with other farmers groups across the country and the world such as the wordwide *Via Campesina*, CLOC (the

Coordinator of Latinamerican Farmers Organisations) and the *Movemento Sem Terra* (Land-less farmers movement) in Brazil.

The main centre of MOCASE in the town of Quimilí houses an impressive infrastructure — a workshop, clinic, office, a community radio which transmits across the local area allegedly paid for by money from leftist Catalan politicians, and an *escuela campesina* (famers school).

This last feature is perhaps the most impressive. Through involvement from the *Universidad de los Transhumantes* (see later), the idea of the farmers' school is to train farmers as teachers, using popular education techniques, so they can teach others from their own communities. Material used would be applicable to their lives rather than teaching specialised knowledge for the modern capitalist labour market. Members of MOCASE also develop workers co-operatives to grow and sell their produce more effectively. In particular, MOCASE set up a central commission of small producers, named 'Ashpa Sumaj' in their native language Quechua, which co-ordinates the production and selling of goods.

MOCASE's work, started with the defence of the land. But this opened up much bigger questions and solutions — co-operative working and producing, popular education, land preservation, self-management and the creation of more humane social relations. Through self reflection, they realised the way they were incorporated into the modern capitalist economy was the problem. Their desire for self management and autonomy came from an understanding that the priorities of the state, insecure land tenure and the

Left, Radio MOCASE
Transmitting from a small prefab structure, Radio MOCASE serves as an information focal point for the local farming community

Right, Ashpa Sumaj
One of the trucks collectively owned by the 'Central Commission of Small Producers' run bt MOCASE

interests and activities of big business were all blocks to a better life for them and their families. The isolation, minimal resources and tough conditions they have faced, make MOCASE an inspiration for popular, autonomous movements all over the world.

POPULAR EDUCATION OPENING THE DOOR TO CHANGE

Tell me and I forget, show me and I learn, involve me and I remember.

HAVING TO SURVIVE HUNGER, unemployment and repression has provided many Argentinians with new resources and ideas. Rather than relying on the state, the church, or the trade union, part of the path of autonomy in Argentina has been popular education. Popular education is different from nearly everything we are taught at school. It is education which connects us with the lives, stories and struggles of people, not a history of elites and their desire for conquest, profit and power. Not a history of the rich few, but the many. It is where teachers become students and students become teachers. It is education which equips people with basic skills so they can organise for themselves rather than learning specialised skills so they can become a cog in the modern money economy.

Latin America has a long tradition of popular education, through pioneering work by people like the Brazilian educator Paulo Friere, who used education as a tool to 'emancipate the oppressed' and to help them understand the world around them on their own terms. Popular education is used extensively throughout Argentina to help people make sense of the current crisis. *Rondas de Pensamiento Autonoma* (roundtables for autonomous discussion), and open platforms in neighbourhood assemblies are common features in Argentina allowing people to engage in a free exchange of ideas about the crisis and possible solutions.

The *Universidad Transhumante* (UT), or Transhumance University, is one such group who is promoting popular education. Their philosophy is based around a rejection of the 'cuadristas' (those who use conventional teaching methods) and support of the Frieristas (those who want to use education as a tool of liberation and autonomy). Originally from the University of San Luis, UT embarked on a year long caravan round Argentina stopping at 80 cities holding popular education workshops to find out what problems faced people across the country. UT has built up a network of volunteers across Argentina who work with autonomous groups who are struggling for social change. In Santiago del Estero, for example, UT is helping MOCASE establish an *Escuela Campesina* (Farmer's School) and with help from the University of San Luis they propose to jointly develop a course entitled Education for Farmers. Here, the farmers of

SUPERMARKET SQUAT. 'EL TIGRE' ROSARIO'S RECLAIMED SUPERMARKET

"Three years ago, if someone had told me we'd be able to run this place I'd never have believed them. I was just a housewife doing a few shifts as a cashier. I believed we needed bosses to tell us what to do, now I realise that together we can do it better then them"

Maria, 56 years old
part of the El Tigre collective

El Tigre supermarket
Among the rambling half-stocked shelves, products from many of Argentina's reoccupied and collectivised factories can be found

MOCASE can gain a qualification and then go on to train other farmers. The idea is to give the farmers struggling for land the skills to teach themselves and further their ability to self manage their lives. UT has also undertaken a Circo Popular (Popular Circus) which brought together theatre, dance and education workshops at Roca Negra in Buenos Aires in late 2003, which aimed to involve people in a shared process of understanding about what is happening in their locality, country and the world.

These types of education, which involve people on equal terms, are the seeds of change — being able to look at the world in different ways, finding solutions to problems with new resources, having the self confidence that people can organise for themselves, and developing a critical language for criticising and evaluating the surrounding world.

MARIA PROUDLY SHOWED US AROUND 'EL TIGRE' pointing out that they stock pastry and pasta from a local reclaimed factory and that as much of their fresh fruit and vegetables as possible is local. Neither of these would have occurred while this shop was part of a large chain.

In the 1990s, Francisco Regunaschi the owner of El Tigre, a local businessman who owned several other supermarkets took out a $3 million mortgage to buy the supermarket. The Argentinian economy began to take a nosedive which, together with the opening of large international hypermarkets like France's Carrefour, made the supermarket less and less profitable. In May 2001 the supermarket

Left, outside El Tigre
'Workers co-operative. Workers in struggle' reads the defiant sign above the entrance to El Tigre supermarket

Centre, collective ravioli
A reoccupied factory Mil Hojas, proudly states on its packaging that "with this purchase you are directly helping an Argentinian firm that has been reoccupied and collectivised by its workers"

was closed with workers owed months of wages, and the owner started the process of bankruptcy. Somehow this has meant the business is bankrupt but not him — handy since he'd just got his hands on so much cash! The closure of the supermarket meant hundreds of people lost their jobs — joining the 30 per cent of Argentina's population who are officially unemployed or sub employed (the unofficial figure is much larger). Initially many of the workers had faith that their boss would not leave them in the lurch, and that he would seek a solution and their jobs would be returned to them.

As the consciousness of the people in Argentina awoke to the fact that businessmen and the fat cats had never looked after them and never would, people began to reclaim responsibility for their lives in many different ways. The ex-workers of El Tigre began by taking back the supermarket car park and reopening it to raise campaign funds. This included a 24-hour picket with a caravan in the car park providing some respite from the cold winter nights. The workers discovered they had a lot of local support from both the local community and students in Rosario. On 27th July 2001, they decided there was no good reason to stay out in the cold and

entered and reclaimed the supermarket building and have been there ever since.

The ex-workers occupied the building with

the intention of reopening the supermarket. However, they realised this would require organisation, start-up funds and time. Ironically, El Tigre was first built by *Hogar Obrero* (Worker's Home) a socialist supermarket chain who, as part of their paternalistic nature, built it complete with an auditorium in the basement and the whole first floor as a large canteen/social space. There was a lot of support and interest in opening the first floor as a social centre to make immediate use of the building — hence *La Toma* (literally the taken) Cultural Centre was opened. The Cultural Centre is used for a wide range of activities from yoga and community assembly meetings to student meetings and theatre workshops. Last year the national meeting of reclaimed businesses was held there with 1,500 people attending over the day. The basement auditorium is also used for political talks, theatre, and puppet shows and houses a library with thousands of donated books. At the end of August 2003, a community café was opened by students from Rosario University, providing cheap food for all.

After getting a loan and support from the trade union AEC, the Association of Commercial Firms, the supermarket finally opened in June 2002. Obviously any stock already in the supermarket was sold — waste not want not! Electricity is currently 'borrowed' from a line running outside the building that originates in a nearby trade union building. They sell locally produced fruit and vegetables, products from reclaimed factories and *mate* (the Argentinian herb drink) from a farmer's collective. This is particularly encouraging as most mate is now a cash

Llegando a dos años de lucha por los puestos de trabajo

La COOPERATIVA DE TRABAJADORES EN LUCHA
re- abre sus puertas a partir del Lunes 30 de Junio.
AHORA CON SERVICIO DE:
Carnicería - Lacteos - Fiambrería - Verdulería
Panadería y artículos de Almacén

TUCUMAN 1349
Nuevo Horario
Lunes a Sábado de 8 a 20 hs.
¡ Los Esperamos

Próximamente apertura del
COMEDOR UNIVERSITARIO

MENÚ ÚNICO
Estudiantes $ 2:20
Público $ 2:60

crop, with growers seeing little of the profits. The supermarket is well used by the local community — partly as it tends to be cheaper, partly as people want to support it as a community resource. It is run collectively through an assembly and all decisions are made jointly involving all staff. Within this there are separate groups such as the group who run La Toma, the purchasers of goods, car park staff etc.

Today's supermarkets are one of the worst examples of a modern economy — owned by a handful of greedy multinationals, run hierarchically, providing unskilled low wage jobs, blighting the local community and killing off local shops, sourcing products from all over the world while tying producers into unfair buying arrangements. El Tigre, whilst not perfect (we saw many products from multinational companies in there including Nestlé), it is radically different from Safeways or Walmart.

It is run pretty horizontally by the workers, forms a useful part of the community by providing cheap food, entertainment and information, has given unemployed workers wages and control over their lives, and stocks local products many of which are produced by other factories reclaimed by unemployed workers.

'EL CALDERO' CENTRO SOCIAL

Argentina, is the land of the tango, you've got to try it, everyone told us. But all the tango nights seemed a bit touristy or over-priced. Then some friends took us to 'El Caldero'. El Caldero (the cauldron) is a squatted social centre in Rosario run by a women's collective. The collective have been in the building four years and have renovated it. The downstairs space is used for trapeze workshops, tango lessons and live music. Upstairs is a living space and also houses LaConjuraTV (see later).

Finally, a tango experience in a place we felt comfortable. The lesson started at 10.00pm, we were the only pupils (far too early for Argentinians to venture out). By the time other people started to arrive we'd got the basic nine steps (just about!). The new arrivals were polite, trying to help us learn but they were in another league so we twirled off to the bar. As the evening progressed, the centre filled with people from the neighbourhood eager to tango the night away. Many told us they had been coming to the centre for years.

El Caldero is one of many squatted buildings in Argentina — many are cultural centres like El Caldero, but there are also residential squats, squatted community centres, squatted bakeries, squatted cafeterias, squatted bookshops and popular universities like the University of Las Madres de Plaza de Mayo. There are even squatted banks — after the economic crisis many foreign banks left leaving lots of lovely big buildings that now house community centres and kitchens and shelters for the homeless. With popular support from many groups, the squats were well protected by their users and local communities, but as repression increases and some middle class folk benefit from economic improvements, support has declined and there have been several evictions.

'TIERRA DEL SUR' CENTRO CULTURAL

One impressive squatted social and cultural centre, Tierra del Sur, sadly met its demise. In La Boca, Buenos Aires' forgotten but rapidly gentrifying dock side area, it had been going one and a half years before they were evicted in May 2003, along with the 30 families in the residential squat next door. Prior to its eviction Tierra del Sur's activities included more then 30 art and skills workshops, after school care for kids, five workers co-ops, bike mending and carpentry workshops, a popular library, free legal advice, printing, sexual health advice, darkroom, theatre and puppet performances, live music events, and a solidarity fair and party with the local community. There are still lots of empty buildings in the area and the group have occupied a new building and are gathering energy to start something new. Unfortunately, a public private partnership called

¡GUERRA EN BUENOS AIRES!

Aníbal Ibarra y el Banco COMAFI (Citi Group) quieren desalojar a la ASAMBLEA LEZAMA SUR y a INDYMEDIA ARGENTINA del ex-Banco Mayo recuperado por los vecinos y vecinas de Barracas.
Ibarra y la Corporación del Sur quieren desalojar al CENTRO CULTURAL Y SOCIAL TIERRA DEL SUR.

UN NUEVO ORDEN MUNDIAL NECESITA UN NUEVO ORDEN BARRIAL

'Corporacion del Sur' is responsible for developing the area for business and tourism and is taking a hard line against squats in the area.

Left, 'War in Buenos Aires!'
"A new world order needs a new neighbourhood order", reads the flyer, warning against squat evictions

Right, Trivenchi cultural centre
Jugglers, clowns and artists gather against the eviction at the Trivenchi cultural centre

TRIVENCHI CULTURAL CENTRE

On a more positive note, another squat that has succ- essfully resisted eviction is the Trivenchi brothers' cultural centre, the home of the Trivenchi circus — an amazing space full of trapezes, high wire, juggling sticks, clown noses and everything circuses require! They have successfully resisted two eviction attempts with much local support and many red noses, the last attempt being on 18th July 2003. They have managed to negotiate a legal agreement with the government and are currently awaiting a decision.

POST-INDUSTRIAL SPACES: ROCA NEGRA

The Quilmes area of Greater Buenos Aires is clear evidence of Argentina's loss of industry and economic demise, marked by empty factories, warehouses and

Roundtable at Roca Negra
During the 'Autonomous January' event in 2004, thousands gathered at Roca Negra to discuss and formulate autonomous politics

Lanus one and half years ago. Roca Negra now doubles as a focal point for local projects and groups and nation wide meetings for autonomous groups from across the country.

Four days after arriving in Argentina, we visited Roca Negra. As part of the commemoration activities for the year anniversary of the Avellaneda massacre, many of the autonomous movements from all over Argentina gathered to share their experiences, give talks, hold workshops, sell collectively made products, display photos, print T-shirts, make food, discuss how to work together and launch two books written by people in the MTD. The event was hosted by the MTD at Roca Negra and, amongst others, groups present included the Mapuche Indians, Buenos Aires Indymedia, AnRed (an alternative media collective), Argentina Arde (an alternative photography collective), various community assemblies, and the farmers of Mocase.

The wealth of Argentina's new popular social

shipyards and unemployment exceeding 50 per cent in places. It's for this reason that MTD Anibal Veron is strong here. Roca Negra, is one such empty industrial site. Once a shipbuilding yard, it now houses a range of autonomous projects, including a community garden, bakery, workshop, pharmacy and meeting space. The building and land came under government ownership when the foreign company pulled out, and they gave the space to the Madres de Plaza de Mayo, who then offered the space to MTD movements represented here was overwhelming — so many stories, photos and discussions gave a strong sense of collectiveness and struggle for autonomy. As we wandered outside the contrast was stark between the decaying post-industrial setting of the collapsing chimneys and piles of industrial rubble, and the colourful organic garden, the bakery and one of the community assemblies singing as they prepared an *olla popular* making a large pan of stew to feed all assembled.

ALTERNATIVE MEDIA SPACES AND COLLECTIVES

23RD JULY 2003. AN INTERVIEW WITH ARGENTINA INDYMEDIA, BUENOS AIRES

After the anti-World Trade Organisation (WTO) actions in Seattle in 1999, several IMCs (Independent Media Centres) were established in the USA, with the first in Seattle. On 1st May 2000, the idea of Indymedia spread across the Atlantic to London. Other European IMCs followed in Italy and France; IMC Prague was set up to cover the anti-World Bank protests on 26th September 2000 in Prague. Three years after the anti-WTO actions in Seattle, there are now more than 100 IMCs across all continents.

Independent media projects are spreading around the planet at unprecedented speed. Triggered by discontent with the mainstream media and supported by the widespread availability of media technologies, groups all over the world are creating their own channels of information and distribution in order to bypass the (mainstream) corporate media. The idea behind most of these projects is to create open platforms to which everyone can contribute — not only a small media elite with their particular interests. By eliminating the classic division between professional producers and passive audience, many issues and discussions that were previously suppressed become visible and available. Below is an interview we did with Indymedia Argentina.

Can you tell us a little bit about the origins of Indymedia Argentina?

Indymedia Argentina emerged from the same group of organisations that work in Europe. To get organised collectively to cover actions against events of multinational organisations like in April 2001 with the Free Trade Area of the Americas. Local people got together here in Buenos Aires with others from the USA and Canada, with the idea of setting up a media centre. We got together with people already working in independent media and from there we set up the web page. We set it up with the idea of covering the meeting here when the ministers were going to sign the Free Trade Agreement of the Americas (FTAA) and from then on, there remained a fairly unstable work group linked to the global social resistance collective that started firstly in Prague

Indymedia Argentina.
Special issue of the Indymedia
Aregentina magazine
commemorating the massacre
of 26th June 2002

group went from six or seven people to fifteen and then thirty. At the same time, in the summer, Indymedia Rosario was started.

And more than this, from this moment publications on the web page exploded. The web page as a newswire transformed itself into a reference point to find accurate information direct from the streets to your house without intermediaries. This is what generated a situation where Indymedia was identified as a tool. Also there has been interest from a huge amount of people, and at the moment we are making video and running independent journalism courses. It was a very hot summer after the events of 20th December 2001.

So Indymedia is much more than the website?

Yeah, totally. If you intended to have a printed newspaper, it would be difficult to reach a wide audience in Argentina. In many ways, the space grew through the communication equipment of the organisations that accessed the site, and they diffused it. It attempts to diffuse a new format with more access to the street where you can publish the information that only circulates by the internet and multiply it.

At the moment in Argentina, why is there a need for independent media?

I think it is well known in Argentina, as in other parts of the world, that media is controlled by multinationals or is in the hands of two or three firms, and when faced with critical moments you find that the inform-

(2000) and also with a network like what you would call 'Global-ise Resistance' that has links with Trotskyist parties. For a while, Indymedia was very focused and from November/December 2001 the

...tion is altered or distorted, or access is limited when the system is put into crisis by demonstrations.

It becomes evident that other motivations are needed, not just considering information as a product like in business. When you stop being a business you change. We have another perspective that is to think of communication from the point of view of social change, or aiming to improve the situation of people in general or for the people who are organising or politicised for this, and so information becomes something very necessary. Also when there are so many people organising, there is a need for an alternative space, and the necessity comes from them.

Before an alternative space is found the massive use of Indymedia begins, because the tool permits active use without filters in contrast to other traditional forms of media. When the political and economic system becomes questioned is when the traditional forms of media begin to retreat and guard their interests, and it is then that the alternative media achieves its fundamental role of offering a space where they can transmit proposals and experiences. They also experience the repression of the media. Independent media correspondents have an important role in that they are in the streets covering the work of the social movements, and they can document and stop a little of the police brutality that you see so often in Argentina — during this so-called democracy, 80 have died and this didn't appear in any papers. For this reason, the mobilisations depend upon independent journalists.

What is the situation here with the media?

The most important media group is Clarín, with interests in papers, radio, TV, mobile communications and shares in others industries. It's one of the largest selling papers in Latin America.

How has the violence affected Indymedia?

On two occasions, once last year, two members of IM were shot with rubber bullets covering a Greenpeace action. To try and stop the activists being detained, there was a demonstration which went to the police station to liberate them. The response from the police was they attacked some of our members, one with a camera and the other with a video camera, both clearly identified as journalists. The other incident was relatively recently in the entrance way of the Brukman factory. This also occurred at the start of a conflict between demonstrators and police, and one Indymedia journalist who had been there for hours taking photos in a place near to the police was hit when they advanced. Knowing that he was a photographer, knowing that he was working as a journalist, various police hit him and he had to be hospitalised. It was a generalised repression, they applied it to everyone there. There were over 100 arrested, including a deputy they kidnapped. The situation with the police is really difficult and complicated and you don't know how they are going to respond. There are very large costs that you have to assume. It changed alot after what happened on 26th June 2002, until then nobody in the police had been reprimanded, but then they realised the effect of the coverage of the repression and the legality of the protesters.

What are the main areas that you cover?

We always cover demonstrations in general and in the streets with the movements of unemployed workers (MTDs), the movement of occupied factories, and that which remains of the movement of neighbourhood assemblies. The work is divided into sections with people specialised in different sectors as featured on the web, each one reflecting different social movements. The office space of Indymedia functions from a neighbourhood assembly building, and also there is an information project working with the MTDs where there are about 20 people working and making media.

What is the role of Indymedia to help the people understand and find solutions for the crisis?

This is a part of the present role which Indymedia undertakes, the challenge that we now confront, is to analyse errors and successes of the movement in general and to see what happens with the new president and his progressive responses. What we are focusing on now is to look at what has been done, systematise the information that there is, show the proposals to the different organisations or people. The problems deep down in the economy and with the fund (International Monetary Fund) still haven't been felt, as with unemployment — in spite of

the slow recuperation of the economy it still reaches levels of 20 per cent. We intend to show alternative proposals to the capitalist system of today.

What is the role of Indymedia in popular education?

Now it's gaining relevance, it's a theme which took hold in the middle of last year and has started to function three months ago with some funds and energy that previously didn't exist to structure and develop workshops. Similarly in Argentina, there is a strong tradition of popular education, but not in respect to the media. Now there's going to be a meeting for popular education here in Buenos Aires in the Faculty of Social Sciences.

Since December 2001 and the killings of 26th June 2002, how has the situation changed here for Indymedia and for social movements?

It put forward radical change, from a state of apathy to widespread looting and protests — with the movement of piqueteros that acquired a very interesting dynamic after the events of December, with the coordination of neighbourhood assemblies and occupied factories, presenting alternatives to capitalist life like expropriation of factories, autonomous neighbourhoods and assemblies.

It began a new spectrum of action and new forms of how to do politics. Neighbourhood assemblies occupying banks, that closed after robbing the people and left with their money. They broke cultural bonds across the organisation of assemblies, llowing people to take action and occupy banks.

The 26th June 2002 was a moment when they wanted to limit the strength of the movement with the planned assassination of two people. The access routes to the Federal Capital remained blocked and the demands were dignified work, education, health and an end to the repression. The government response led to the loss of two key compañeros for the movement and the people acquired a consciousness of everything involved in the generation of the movement, that it is not only blocking roads, but also the work in the neighbourhoods making libraries, people's kitchens, work for the young. All of this is compatible with the work of Indymedia.

And after these events, was there much repression?

It's difficult to know. In the poor neighbourhoods the effect was very strong. The movement was to an extent paralysed. On the other hand, it served to make other sectors of society conscious of what happened, there were massive demonstrations, and from all the sectors of society, not only the margins.

Many eyes in Europe are fixed on Argentina, due to the new responses being generated to the problems of neoliberalism. In your opinion what is the state of the popular rebellion now and in what way will it develop?

I don't know, it's a moment of reflection, this social calm to see what we do well and what we do badly. At first it was very radical, a lot of anger, there were impressive acts of civil disobedience. Everything came from the confrontations, the violence was legitimate. Then divisions started to occur within the movement generated by frustrations and the slowness of change. In the poor neighbourhoods, there remained prepared local structures.

At the moment, the government has distanced itself from Menemism and neoliberalism, but there are still problems. What are the challenges for the future?

We have to find new ways to maintain the structures and institutions which have risen up, but in the middle of material problems which the people can't solve, I don't know how a government with a different direction will affect their survival. Its something similar to what happened in Brazil with Lula, that the left came, but now he's best friends with Bush. So we have to see what will happen with Kirchner.

He is trying to do positive things, for example in relation to the judiciary. But there are deep seated questions that we have to see answered like what will happen to an independent judiciary when they start to affect people that helped him in his political campaign, the people that own large firms; this is all very linked in Argentina. If you want to investigate crimes, you always arrive at the president, like the crime at the AMIA [Argentinian Jewish Association], how far are you going to go when you discover that Duhalde's police are involved, that it was him who helped Kirchner in his campaign. My position is that we are not going to advance much, that we are going to stay here.

What are the challenges for the future for Argentina?

It's complicated. I can't speak for the people! I hope for the construction of autonomy, to focus on a more co-operative life and for self management. That power leaves us alone at the margins to be able to construct is good, I don't believe in the logic of confrontation for the sake of confrontation, so let's see what happens. To recover lost illusions for a lot of people that have been cheated. It's obvious that the system doesn't offer alternatives, in the long term it can't solve the fundamental problems, the only thing it can produce is pollution and hunger. To offer an alternative and to advance and coordinate territorial and distributional organisations. Also we have to advance at the level of Latin America.

PLANETA X COLLECTIVE

"The future is now. It is experience that develops us. Everyday we produce the future, in every instant we discover an idea of the future. The future is the multiplication of new types of space, where other principles reign, where other emotions are produced, work is organised in new forms, happiness. We don't want a market-led world, with all its miseries and anguish, we are the other world, we are inventing it here and now, in this space where we meet and we do things together. This is the sentiment of our practice."

Pretty amazing words, but then so is the space and the people at Planeta X in Rosario. They are an arts collective that started in 1995 doing poetry, theatre and video. Planeta X is a space in a rented building, it is the collective and it is the events they put on, which vary from full-on banging club nights to chilled Sunday afternoon music sessions. They also develop experimental music and multimedia performances. Indymedia Rosario is also based in one of the rooms in the house.

In 1999, they became an organised collective holding open weekly meetings, and in March 2001 they developed their own space to put on a number of events including a fortnightly club night. One of the collective members told us how important horizontal and equal organising is:

"The meetings are assemblies. In the assemblies the principle is horizontality. Horizontality is the opposite of

hierarchy. Anyone can say, propose, think, do what they want. Nobody except everyone has any power over anything or anyone" (or as they say more eloquently in Castillian — Nadie excepto todos tiene ninguna autoridad sobre nada ni nadie).

PIRATE TV. LACONJURA

Pirate radio stations are a familiar part of DIY culture, but a group in Argentina went one further with a pirate TV channel which broadcast briefly across Buenos Aires. During their brief time broadcasting in Buenos Aires, the pirate TV station built up much support but they didn't have enough material to broadcast continuously. When the government found them, they didn't have enough support to stop the inevitable arrests.

Inspired by this pirate TV channel, we visited the La Conjura collective in Rosario that has been doing alternative media work for a number of years, like video and photography. Learning from the experience of the Buenos Aires collective, LaConjura decided to spend some time preparing material and building up grassroots support in Rosario. They put out a monthly video documenting, tongue in cheek, incidents which occurred during the uprising and subsequent repression, as well as making more TV style pieces of work that combine political reporting with comedy sketches, spoof ads and talk shows and their own soap opera featuring Rosario's best known homeless person. The videos are then shown all over Rosario, with an anti-copyright policy to encourage distribution. Whether LaConjura starts broadcasting

as a pirate TV station or not, their footage is reaching a wide audience and forms an important part of the independent media scene.

RECLAIMED FACTORIES

'Without the bosses the factories work, but without the workers...'

WHEN THE PESO WAS PEGGED TO THE DOLLAR in 1991, Argentinian products and workers became expensive. Soon factories and businesses were closing by the dozen leaving millions unemployed. Used to being at the rough end of the global economy, many Argentinian workers have reclaimed factories and businesses ranging from 5-star hotels and pastry factories to metal works. Each factory or business has its own story, but what they have in common is that most organise using assemblies and flat structures to make decisions. Trying to secure their futures has occurred in different ways. Two different routes are used: either the formation of legally recognised workers co-operatives or seeking nationalisation through government expropriation but with the factory remaining under worker's control. Many of the re-occupied factories are coordinated through two organisations: the National

Movement of Recovered Factories which has 3,600 workers across 60 factories, and the National Federation of Workers Co-operatives in Recovered Factories which has 1,447 across 14.

The obvious question for us was why would the workers want to control a factory that still holds them within the global economy and a culture of consumerism, and why they would choose to be nationalised by a government nobody can trust. The answer lies in survival. In a country where 60 per cent of people live below the poverty line, unemployment in some of the poorer areas of Buenos Aires verges on 100 per cent, people have no land to provide for themselves and there is no food for their children. In these circumstances reclaiming a factory or business, running it autonomously and horizontally, and everyone getting fair wages (rather then none or derisory ones) is an empowering and life improving activity. And reclaimed factories have begun to move away from uncritical commodity production. Brukman Textiles, for example have tried to alter what they produce from luxuries to essentials by suggesting that they could make work clothes for the health services if they were nationalised rather than just expensive tailored suits. The choice to be nationalised with local workers control rather then forming an independent workers co-operative is also a pragmatic response. Nationalisation offers a chance of survival and access to markets and capital. With nationalisation also comes access to government schools, hospitals and other services which smaller factories might be unable to provide.

HOTEL BAUEN. 5-STAR WORKERS' POWER

Hotel Bauen sits on one of the principal routes in Buenos Aires, Avenida Callao; its 20 storeys look across the city. The previous 5-star hotel costing $US100 per night was closed in 2001, presumably through lack of custom. The business went bankrupt and now owes money to various creditors and hence there is no overall control of the defunct hotel. The picture is further confused as the old owner died and his sons are reluctant to get involved in this debt ridden venture.

Enter the workers and the popular rebellion. Lying empty for two years, the hotel was reoccupied by the workers in Easter 2003 who are preparing to reopen it, possibly in late 2003. Forty of the original workers are negotiating with the govern-ment to reopen the hotel and are looking into a loan to buy all the supplies they need. This loan, it was suggested, wouldn't have fixed repayments but would depend on the success of the hotel. One member told us that it will reopen on a much smaller scale, probably 3-star, but would have a wider appeal and would include a cultural/ community centre. In terms of clientele, Bill Gates isn't welcome, but instead they aim to target social clientele — trades unions, charities, social movement groups, community workers as well as sympathetic tourists. The workers were keen to go it alone, in part because they were left without support from their union, Gastronomics, during the closure of the hotel. In an effort to work more co-operatively, the workers have aligned themselves with the more horizontal MTD.

NUESTRA LUCHA (OUR STRUGGLE).
THE BRUKMAN TEXTILE WORKERS, BUENOS AIRES

On a cold street corner beneath colourful banners proclaiming 'Workers of Brukman resisting — not one step back' a group of men and women of various ages huddle round a drum fire drinking mate. Sharing mate is a quintessential sign of comradeship. This traditional Argentinian herbal drink is passed around rapidly. The 'mate' is fashioned from a gourd made from a small squash plant and using the bombilla (a metal straw) each person takes a suck and passes it back to the owner who adds more hot water from a flask or kettle and passes it on to the next person in the circle. To pass the cold evening, they welcome their new foreign guests eagerly and we swap stories of politicians, footballers and police confrontations. Behind the fire there are several small tents and in front a large canvas marquee containing a few camp beds, a heater and several sewing machines.

Many workers had been holding a 'macinazo' in the street. Denied access to their workplace, they continue to work in the street, making garments for people affected by a flood in Santa Fe, a region to the north. Inside we are greeted by a young man eager to tell us their story, of how they — 50 workers — reopened and ran their own textile factory and how this attracted brutal state repression including a violent eviction over the Easter weekend in 2003. This is the Brukman camp, sat on a street corner half a block from the Brukman textile factory which is now closely guarded by a line of riot police. The workers and supporters were living at the camp here whilst they pursued legal and other channels to once again reclaim their factory. They have hosted cultural events and it is a permanent signal that the Brukman workers are far from giving up their factory.

The Brukman textile factory was for a year or so one of over 200 reclaimed factories in Argentina. In December 2001 the workers reached the end of their patience with the owners, as over the previous months their wages had been reduced, further reduced and then not paid. They gathered to demand their wages and the owner and foreman said they

Not one step back!
The defiant camp outside the Brukman textile factory in Buenos Aires, where workers were regularly and violently evicted by the police in 2003

The macinazo
The Brukman women continue sewing in the streets, making clothes for flood victims in northern Argentina

Left, a Brukman eviction
*Police violently evict the
Brukman workers during
Easter 2003*

Centre, victory at last
*Joyous workers gather at the
news that they have won the
right to own and manage the
Brukman factory*

meetings. Workers shared the night guard duty. After successfully running the factory for a year and four months the workers suffered a brutal eviction on the Thursday night before the Easter weekend of 2003 whilst only four workers were present.

Despite support from up to 20,000 people including workers of other reclaimed businesses, community assemblies and unemployed workers movements, the attempt to retake the factory which lasted the whole weekend and into the following week and resulted in many injuries and 130 arrests, was unsuccessful. Since then the workers have been camped on the next corner with the factory permanently under police guard. Over the six days of resistance, those present came under attack from water canons, tear gas, and plastic bullets with the police using motorbikes and helicopters to track the crowd.

When we visited the camp outside the factory in July 2003, the Brukman workers were pursuing a claim for expropriation of the factory and were forming a legal co-operative with the aspiration to run the factory under workers control but nationalized. This is how a number of the reclaimed factories are managed giving them legal export licenses, guaranteed minimum salaries and access to health and education services, and with the added bonus that the government takes on the owner's debts. After such a bitter struggle, the workers were not ruling out other more direct channels to take back the factory.

Events took another downturn. On 25th September 2003, there was a hearing by the commercial court to decide the future of the Brukman factory and whether to declare the original company

would return soon with the cash, but as night fell there was no sign of the employers. Some of the workers stayed in the factory overnight. The owners, it turns out, had gone for good leaving debts to everyone from gas and electricity to unpaid social insurance. The workers realized that the owners had gone but decided to carry on making their high quality suits without bosses and time sheets but with wages, direct democracy and cooperation.

Over the next few months they paid off some of the utility bills and repaired sewing machines, and even found money to pay a nurse's salary to ensure on site medical attention. Sacked workers were traced to increase staff and the work atmosphere changed completely with Bolivian folk music and laughter rather than silence as the soundtrack to work. Cultural events were put on in the factory such as film showings and space was offered for

ankrupt. This decision had major implications for
the Brukman workers as the government previously
stated that it would only expropriate the factory and
its contents if the company was declared bankrupt.
There was a complete turn around with the judge
deciding to prosecute six of the Brukman workers
for 'usurpation' and widen the investigation to see if
any further workers should be prosecuted. They also
proposed to give the factory back to the owners,
allowing them to pay off their debts at devalued
rates despite their numerous crimes such as
inventing debts to themselves, tax evasion and
absence of accounts.

On 1st October, a further march demanding
expropriation of the building went to the government
offices. Delegates from the Brukman workers group
then met the legislators and tried to persuade them
to grant expropriation despite the lack of a bankruptcy
decision using the example of the Grissinopolis
factory (a reclaimed breadstick factory) where
expropriation was granted without a bankruptcy
agreement. The legislators agreed to continue the
debate. The current chapter in the Brukman story
ended suddenly and
triumphantly on 31st
October, when the
factory was legally
expropriated to the
workers who now,
through a legal co-
operative, run and
own the factory and
the machines.

ZANON CERAMICS, NEUQUÉN. BAJO CONTROL OBRERO (UNDER WORKERS CONTROL)

"In a rich country and a province full of resources, the workers and the people have suffered unemployment, poverty, low wages, homelessness, lack of education and healthcare. The workers produce the riches, therefore we must believe in our own strength. In our hands lies the solution and the future. Zanon belongs to the people".

In the Neuquén
province, 1500km south
of Buenos Aires lies
the Zanon ceramics
factory. It is one of
South America's
biggest, with the
capacity to produce a
million square metres
of ceramics per month.
Throughout 2000, the
workers were in
dispute with the
owners over pay cuts. In 2001, the owners shut the
factory sacking 380 workers, but the workers started
a campaign to reopen it under workers control. With
massive local support, the factory was reopened
under worker's control in January 2002. Initially it
operated on a smaller scale but with all workers
guaranteed a wage of 800 pesos a month. This was
agreed by the assembly of workers, using a

Zanon Ceramics
Above the factory gates, a sign reads "Zanon Ceramics is the workers"

Left, a workers' assembly
Workers gather on the factory
floor and debate the running of
Zanon Ceramics

Right, bajo control obrero
Finished ceramic tiles awaiting
distribution are stamped with
the powerful message "under
workers' control!"

horizontal decision making process which allows all to have a say. This is how all decisions are made. Commissions were set up to manage Sales, Administration, Security, Planning, Purchasing, Hygiene and Sanitation, Press, Diffusion, and Production. There have since been three further incorporations of workers (all ex-Zanon workers) — all of whom start on the same salary as other workers and have a voice and vote in the assemblies. The factory, with 270 workers, is now producing 120,000 metres squared per month, 20 per cent of the total capacity and 50 per cent of what was being produced before the factory was abandoned.

The reclaimed factory has strong community links, donating money to hospitals, schools, and other local services, selling tiles at cost price to people in Neuquén so that dirt floors could be tiled,

putting on social and cultural events such as films, performances, art exhibitions and doing their own solidarity actions with a wide range of groups including the unemployed workers movements, other occupied factories, teachers and health workers. They now have their own doctors, psychologists and other health professionals working on site. They also have close links with the Mapuches, one of Argentina's few remaining indigenous groups, and support their land right struggle. Such solidarity is reciprocated. When one of Zanon's clay suppliers refused to supply the factory as it was under workers control the Mapuches stepped in and started supplying the clay. There are now four ceramics lines called Mapuche with their traditional symbols on them.

There have been four eviction attempts by the

tate and police — all violent and repressive. All have
ailed due to resistance from the workers and large
upport from the community. There have also been
personal attacks with kidnapping of workers and
wages stolen. At the last eviction attempt in April
'003 there was support from the MTDs, the Madres
le Plaza de Mayo, various other unemployed
workers movements, NGOs, church groups,
secondary school kids and various local community
assemblies and groups.

On 17th October 2002, the Zanon workers
submitted a proposal for expropriation of the factory
with no compensation, for the factory to run legally
under workers control and for it to be nationalised.
The worker's assembly chose a delegation to go to
Buenos Aires to talk with the Government and the
judge. However, the judge insists that the trade
union bosses, Picado and Levy, take joint possession
of the factory — a situation that the workers
obviously cannot accept. The workers continue to
push for expropriation and say they will not be forced
to compromise the way they work, the jobs they have
created and that they have no faith in those who have
been trying to evict them (largely the trade
unionists). One worker summed it up:

*"Only with our struggle can we find a solution and
twist the arm of those who until now work to defend
the interests of the owners. Whilst we continue to
negotiate we must continue production and the
struggle".*

**IMPA CULTURAL CITY. LUCHA, TRABAJO, CULTURA
(STRUGGLE, WORK, CULTURE)**

To give yourself form
To reform yourself
To deform yourself
To navigate without witchcraft
To look at the work of an anthill
To understand the gestures of a baby
To draw with your eyes closed
To be able to invent a word for something that doesn't exist
To be able to think of a colour that you've never seen
To imagine the face of the child you don't have
To make words live
To count the hairs on your head
To guess a name
To guess a man
To read a language that you don't know
To draw an entire line
To say our miseries in a raised voice
To love
To create a spectacle
To forgive
To struggle daily
To understand
To understand yourself
To listen to ideas
To find the words
To make ideas
To change your thoughts
To change the world

Left, IMPA cultural centre
The programme of events and workshops of IMPA's cultural centre range from photojournalism to trapeze and dance classes

Right, "No peace for the killers"
"If there isn't justice, there's escrache", reads a poster for an escrache against General Olea in the suburbs of Buenos Aires in June 2003

IMPA (Industrias Metalúrgicas y Plásticas Argentinas) is a large metallurgic factory in Buenos Aires. In 1961, it became a co-operative, although at times this was more in name than character. With the economic decline of the late 1990's more and more workers were laid off. In 1995 there were 500 workers and by late 1997 when the process of bankruptcy was initiated there were only 50 workers left. The last to be laid off refused to accept the situation and rejected the administration group's decision to close the factory. A workers assembly took the decision to reclaim the factory. They slowly got the factory back up and running — getting utilities reconnected and sourcing raw materials. Now, five years later they are paying the workers $900 pesos a month rather than only $5, incorporating new workers and even have export orders.

An important part of IMPA is its cultural centre — the Cultural City. The writing above is taken

"IN BETWEEN SETS OF THE MOST AMAZING ARGENTINIAN AND BOLIVIAN FOLK MUSIC I HAVE EVER HEARD I NIP TO THE TOILET. ON MY LATE-NIGHT JOURNEY, I PASS ROLLS OF ALUMINIUM TWICE MY HEIGHT, RAILS MOVING METAL OBJECTS AROUND THE FACTORY AND LOTS OF PEOPLE AT WORK. THEY ALL SMILE AND SAY HELLO, AND ON THEIR BREAKS THEY COME AND LISTEN TO OR WATCH THE VARIOUS EVENTS IN THE CULTURAL SPACES. THEY GET TO DO ANY CLASS OR GO TO ANY EVENT FOR FREE. WHEN I RETURN SOMEONE HAS MOUNTED THE TRAPEZE AND IS PROVIDING ADDITIONAL ENTERTAINMENT! LOOKING AROUND AT THE OTHER PEOPLE SPENDING THEIR FRIDAY NIGHT IN THE IMPA CULTURAL CENTRE, THEY ARE AN ECLECTIC CROWD FROM ALL WALKS OF LIFE. DEFINITELY A INSPIRING CULTURAL SPACE IN TERMS OF WHAT IS ON OFFER AND CHALLENGING THE (FALSE) DIVISION OF WORK AND PLAY."

from its programme and hints at how they have tried to weave together a traditional working environment with a place of creativity. As interest grew in the reclaimed factory a range of visitors came and one asked to put on a theatre production. This was the start of what is now one of Buenos Aires' most exciting radical social spaces. Currently there are over 20 workshops on offer from circus skills and glasswork, to folk dancing, Quechua writing (one of the indigenous languages) to community mental health. Every week there are at least two drama or dance productions and a music night. They also put on art exhibitions and have artists' studios. In IMPA, art and culture meet production and work, as theatre goers mingle with workers bashing aluminium plates.

PEOPLE'S JUSTICE FOR HUMAN RIGHTS

ESCRACHE. POPULAR JUSTICE FOR A DIRTY WAR

WE LIVE IN A SOCIETY WHERE WE DON'T EXPECT too much in terms of justice but the story of Argentina's dirty war is truly shocking by anyone's standards. 30,000 were officially disappeared and tortured during 1976–83. We may never know the real figure. Argentina has had many military dictatorships but this last one from 1976–83 was the most brutal and devastating. In an attempt to stem rebellion (in the 1970s many guerrilla and left wing

groups grew in Argentina such as the *Montoneros* — literally the numerous ones) and control and terrify the population, anyone involved in 'subversive' activity was disappeared and then held in detention centres, tortured and many finally murdered in grotesque ways including being dropped alive into Buenos Aires' River Plata.

The third military junta was ousted from power when the Malvinas war was lost to the British. A façade of retribution was initiated when two of the most notorious dictators — Videla and Galtieri — went to prison, but many others faced impunity. In 1986, the law of the Final Point (Punta Final) was passed that banned further penal actions against both military and civilians for crimes committed during the dictatorship. *Ley de Obendiencia Debida*

Left, the escrache
Posters against the murder pile up in the Plaza 'Madres de Pañuelo Blanco'

(The Law of Military Obedience) was also passed by the national congress in 1987, exempting from blame all subordinates for the human rights violations during the dictatorship. Then in October 1989, President Menem pardoned several military officials including those involved in the coup that ended democracy back in 1976; and then in December 1990, he pardoned the heads of the military Junta (who had been jailed in 1985 — but held under luxury house arrest). These laws were actually revoked in 1998 but with no retrospective action.

So, few of those actually responsible have been locked up or received any form of retribution. Hence it is clear that official justice is something most Argentinians don't readily expect from their government. Enter the 'escrache' — popular autonomous justice, the meaning of which is to 'expose' or 'uncover'. HIJOS (which literally means children but stands for *Hijos por la Identidad y la Justica contra la Olvido y el Silencio* or 'Children for identity and justice

campaign is started in his area to inform local residents and businesses of the crimes committed by their local resident. This normally leads to the development of local campaign groups who then inform more and more people in the area. Posters are put up, he is refused entry to many local shops, shouted at whilst walking his dog — and then comes the escrache. Well publicised for months before, several hundreds, and often thousands, gather to march to the house of the guilty. It is a lively affair with drums, puppets, banners and great songs.

Centre, marching to the murderer's house
On the march, the group HIJOS carry their banner towards the house of General Olea

Right, en route to General Olea
Human rights and student groups carry banners, one declaring "Prison for the murderer Olea"

and against the forgotten and the silence) is an organisation of sons and daughters and families of those that disappeared in the dirty war. They campaign for information about what happened to their relatives and justice for those responsible. Along with other campaign groups they make up the *Mesa de Escrache*, who organise the escraches.

An escrache is the culmination of months of local campaigning. After someone responsible for acts of genocide in Argentina has been located a

Today we came to 'escrachar' him
To a soldier called Olea
Who's been hiding for a while
Within the neighbood of Saavedra
The years have passed
And the repressors remain free
Carry on murdering
And carry on leaving new corpses

This year the escraches won't end
Oh oh oh!
The people don't forget, they won't be silenced
Oh oh oh!
Repressors don't let down your guard
Nobody wants you
They are killers
They are the shame of Argentina

This is one of the songs we sang on an escrache of General Olea, who ran a detention centre in Neuquén in southern Argentina and is responsible for the torture and death of many of the disappeared. Hundreds of people gathered in a park a kilometre from his house. After an hour or so wait to make sure all stragglers had arrived, we set off in the direction of his house — occupying the road en route. There was dancing, singing and leafleting as we weaved our way towards his house. There was an impressive quantity of flyposting in the local area with information of Olea's crimes and of the planned escrache. As we approached his house, bright yellow road signs were put up marking the distance to his house: "200m to the house of a mass murderer", "100m to the house of a mass murderer". It was obvious when we reached his road judging by the crowd of riot police (there to protect the murderer, who has fled for the day, knowing that this is no ordinary Saturday). The pavement outside and walls were decorated with slogans such as "here lives a murderer", or "30,000 disappeared" and paint bombs were thrown at the house. His next-door-neighbours appear to make it clear they are not happy to discover they share their balcony with a torturer and murderer. After more singing and shouting the crowd disperses peacefully — mission achieved — General Olea is not living in peace.

The feeling of empowerment on this kind of event is incredible, especially in a country where the people have every reason to feel frustrated and power-less. Local campaigning and escraches have been very successful. These murderers and torturers discover that they cannot forget the past, they cannot refuse to take responsibility for their despicable acts. Many have moved — only to be re-escrached. As one chant says: "If there's no justice, there's escrache".

TAKING ON THE MURDERERS. LAS MADRES DE PLAZA DE MAYO
One of the most visible groups striving for justice and against impunity in Argentina is the *Madres de Plaza de Mayo* — literally the Mothers of the May Plaza. These mothers, grandmothers and other relatives began to gather in the Plaza de Mayo, the main square in Buenos Aires in front of the seat of

government, in 1976 as a symbolic act of defiance at the disappearance of their children. Every Thursday at 3.30pm the Madres, wearing their distinctive *pañuelos blancos* (white headscarves), gather in the Plaza and hold their vigil. During some of the worst repression the Madres couldn't meet, but nearly thirty years later they are still there and they have gained massive popular support throughout the country and the world, demanding justice for those disappeared and tortured during Argentina's dictatorship and dirty war.

When asked why they met in the plaza rather than working through other groups, they responded:

We didn't feel very comfortable in other organisations, there was always a desk in the middle, there was always more bureaucracy. But in the plaza we were all equal. They had taken children from all of us, the same thing had happened to all of us, we had been to the same place. And it was like there wasn't any type of difference or distance between us.

The impact of the Madres has gone far wider. On the Plaza del Congreso in the centre of Buenos Aires stands 'La Universidad Popular Madres de Plaza de Mayo', the people's university dedicated to popular education. It houses Buenos Aires' best bookshop on politics, social movements, poetry and popular struggles, the literary café Osvaldo Bayer, gallery and a workshop which holds classes, seminars and debates on topics from across Latin America. In the short space of time we were there, debates were held on the future of Cuban politics, the situation in Venezuela and indigenous rights in Argentina. Many of the Madres, such as their President Hebe de Bonafini, have become outspoken firebrands and comment-ators on life and politics in modern day Argentina and Latin America, making appearances and talking at the end of each Thursday march, at gatherings of neighbourhood assemblies and piqueteros. During the anniversary blockade at Avelleneda, the Madres spoke passionately about the need for justice and the end of impunity for the military copula.

THE ONGOING DESIRE FOR JUSTICE AND AGAINST FORGETTING

The desire for justice and the end to impunity runs deep in Argentina, and is something most can agree on. However, there is a long way to go. On 30th July 2003, countless groups gathered in the main Plaza in Buenos Aires against proposed Government legisla-tion to make protest an act of sedition — in effect criminalise all protest. People on the demo said that in such an inhumane economic system, the right to protest and demand basic rights such as food, shelter and work was even more necessary. Challenging inequality in the street is the only option left for many.

The desire against forgetting runs deep. One afternoon in Rosario during the Guerra Sucia of the 1970s, two friends arranged to meet on a street corner. When Fernando arrived, the only evidence of his friend was his old bicycle leaning against the wall

KEEPING UP THE MOMENTUM of popular power and staying committed to community-based, autonomous politics is difficult. During the uprising the government and the media attempted to demonise the working classes as thugs and vandals who were mindlessly looting supermarkets. This was a tactic to create fear and undermine solidarity between different groups. But enough people stood behind the unemployed and went with them onto the streets to bring down the president and break the status quo. Manipulation by trade unions was also evident. Many trade unions refused to back the protests in December 2001, or chose separate locations to protest. Many people also say that a 'state of ungovernability' was engineered by the Peronist party by December 2001, then in opposition, to get the ruling Alliance Party out of power.

Its also important not to see the uprising as a one off event. Many look to the events of December 2001 as spontaneous. But this robs the events of its history. While many people did go out onto the streets that night in reaction to the state of emergency, the popular uprising was also part of an ongoing popular struggle against centralisation, the state and bosses. The uniqueness of the uprising, then, comes from a potent coming together of the spontaneous uprising of middle class groups with the longer term organising of the working class and

— evidence of when he was last alive. His friend was never seen again. Fernando, left wondering and fearing the worse in the afternoon sun, vowed not to let his friend go unknown. He painted 350 bicycles around the city, to represent the 350 people of Rosario who disappeared in the Dirty War. Each bike has an individual number; each bike is a reminder of pain, of love, and against forgetting.

unemployed. During the most intense mass mobilisations on 19th and 20th December, some of the most inspiring features were the absence of organised unions and the presence of women and young unemployed workers.

What we have learned from Argentina is that politics isn't something which is done far from where you live. For us and them, it is about justice, self-organising, mutual aid and solidarity — in each community, family and workplace. It is about developing and living concrete alternatives to modern life under the capitalist economy, and it is also about making protest a part of everyday existence. Its about remaking the revolution everyday — or as the Zapatistas in Chiapas say it's *"caminar preguntando"* (to walk asking). This is the radical challenge we saw in Argentina – the story of which we have brought home to inspire ourselves and others into action.

How do you maintain the momentum in the long term? How do you keep people believing that they can organise their own lives, for the better? These questions are the ones at the front of many people's minds in Argentina. The same old mixture of complacency, restoring normality, self interest, fear and insecurity and police repression makes many people retreat back into their well trodden social roles. But many Argentinians remain involved in, and committed to, a great diversity of autonomous and collective projects. As the uprising, the deaths and the conflicts fade, its legacy lives on through community kitchens, brick workshops, bakeries, occupied factories, afterschool clubs,

roundtable discussions, puppet shows, jokes and stories. A final voice, to remind us to keep walking, comes from one member of the Unemployed Workers Movement of Solano:

I don't think December 2001 was a lost opportunity for revolution nor was it a failed revolution. It was and is part of the ongoing revolutionary process here. We have learnt many lessons about collective organising and strength, and the barriers to self management. For many people it opened their eyes to what we can do together, and that taking control of our lives and acting collectively whether it's as part of a piquete, a communal bakery or an afterschool club dramatically improves the quality of our lives. If the struggle stays autonomous and with the people the next uprising will have strong foundations to build upon...

GETTING INVOLVED

SOLIDARITY WORK IN ARGENTINA IS NOT EASY or straightforward. There is no central point or organisation to help people who want to get involved. There is also no lack of skills, ideas or enthusiasm within groups and individuals in Argentina so it is often difficult to turn up and fit in. Many groups have been struggling and organising for years and so don't need external support.

However, most groups are welcoming to outsiders, and usually eager to share their stories and allow people to spend a short amount of time with them — if you are politically and culturally sensitive, don't appear like a journalist and are genuinely interested in their struggle and community. Being a vegetarian can be a big problem in Argentina where the standard meal usually consists of some meat. A good knowledge of Spanish is useful and will help you make contacts easier. In the larger cities, many people do speak English — but don't rely on it.

Groups that do take people for longer periods include:

NEIGHBOURHOOD ASSEMBLIES
These are always a good starting point. They are full of information about groups, events, gigs, music, political discussions, and what is going on in the neighbourhood. A short walk around Buenos Aires and you will discover several.

MOCASE
This farmers group has an accompaniment scheme where people can stay in rural communities in the province of Santiago de Estero and help with daily life and be present as human rights observers during land disputes if needed.

MTDs
Although there is no formal way to participate, the unemployed workers groups may welcome people for a week or two, especially if you have a specific skill to share. Contact individual MTDs.

INDYMEDIA
The various independent media centres in Argentina always appreciated visits and help with translations.

The websites on the following page will help you to contact various groups. The best policy is to make personal contacts and take it from there. It may be better to just go to Argentina with plenty of time to spare and make contacts there. Opportunities will vary according to time of year and the political situation. Fundraising and donations for specific projects such as a bakery or workshop is always helpful.

WEBSITES AND EMAIL

Argentina Autonomist Project
www.autonomista.org

Buenos Aires Herald (English news)
www.buenosairesherald.com/

COPA (Co-ordinator of Popular Autonomous Organisations) *http://ar.geocities.com/copa_nacional/*

Counter Culture Magazine
www.contracultural.com.ar/

CounterInformation
www.argentinaarde.org

Guardian Argentina Website
www.guardian.co.uk/argentina/

History of IMPA
www.ciudad.com.ar/ar/portales/cotidiano/nota/0,3104,45219,00.asp

IMPA
www.impa-lafabrica.com.ar/

Indymedia Argentina
www.argentina.indymedia.org

Madres de la Plaza de Mayo
www.madres.org

Marabunta for Popular Power and Social Change
www.marabunta.8k.com/

MOCASE
mocase@hotmail.com

Movimiento de Trabajadores Desocupados
http://ar.geocities.com/movtrabdesoc/

MTD Anibal Veron
www.inventati.org/mtd

MTD Solano
www.solano.mtd.org.ar

Nuestra Lucha — Newspaper of Brukman workers
www.nuestralucha.org/

Planeta X
www.pxweb.com.ar

Red Network News
www.anred.org

Southern News Collective (in Spanish)
www.proyectoconosur.com.ar/Noticias/NoticiaMuestra.asp?Id=1954

Up-to-date list of reclaimed factories
www.lavaca.org/notas/nota248.shtml

Zanon Ceramics
www.obrerosdezanon.org

Z Net
www.zmag.org/argentina_watch.htm

Z Net Latin America
http://zmag.org/LAM/zargentina.html

SOME FURTHER READING

Altvater, E et al (1991) *The Poverty of Nations: A Guide to the Debt Crisis — from Argentina to Zaire*, Zed, London.

Amnesty International (1987) *Argentina, the military juntas and human rights: report of the trial of the former junta members*, 1985, London.

Bethell, L (1993) *Argentina since independence*, Cambridge University Press, Cambridge.

Brysk, A (1994) *The Politics of Human Rights in Argentina: Protest, Change and Democratization*, Stanford University Press, Stanford.

Crassweller, Robert D (1987) *Perón and the enigmas of Argentina*, Norton, London.

Feitlowitz, M (1998) *A Lexicon of Terror: Argentina and the Legacies of Torture*, OUP, New York.

Freire, P (1970) *Pedagogy of the Oppressed*, Penguin, London.

Graham, C and Masson, P (2003) Between politics and economics: The IMF and Argentina, *Current History* 102 (661), pp.72–76.

Harman, C (2002) Argentina: rebellion at the sharp end of the world crisis, *International Socialism Journal* Issue 94.

Jordon and Whitney, J (2002) *Argentina's popular uprising: que se vayan todos*, Parts 1 & 2, February/July.

Keeling, DJ (1996) *Buenos Aires: Global Dreams, Local Crises* (World Cities Series), Wiley, Chichester.

Keeling, DJ (1997) *Contemporary Argentina: A Geographical Perspective*, Westview Press, Oxford.

Lewis, C (2002) *Argentina: a Short History*, One World Publications, London.

Lewis, CM. (1993) *Argentina in the Crisis Years. London: Latin American Studies*.

Moyano, MJ (1995) *Argentina's Lost Patrol: Armed Struggle 1969–1979*, Yale University Press, London.

Munck, R et al (1987) *Argentina: From Anarchism to Peronism 1855–1985*, Zed, London.

Nouzeilles, G (2003) *The Argentina Reader*, Duke University Press, London.

Schamis, HE (2002) Argentina: Crisis and democratic consolidation, *Journal of Democracy* 13 (2), pp.81–94.

IN SPANISH

Alfredo Eric Calcagno y Eric Calcagno (2003) Argentina: Derumbe neoliberal y proyecto nacional, *Le Monde Diplomatique*, Capital Intelectual SA.

Enrique Carpintero y Mario Hernandez (2002) *Produciendo Realidad, Las empresas comunitarias*, Topia editorial.

Francisco Ferrara (2003) *Màs Allà Del Corte De Rutas — La lucha por una Nueva Subjetividad*.

Kohan, A (2002) *A las Calles. Una historia de los movimientos piqueteros y carceroleros de los 90s al 2002*, Colihue, Buenos Aires.

Movimiento de Trabajadores Desocupados Anibal Veron (2003) Dario y Maxi, *Dignidad piquetero*, Ediciones 26 de Junio.

Zibechi, Raul (2003) Genealogía de al revuelta, Argentina: la sociedad en movimiento, La Plata: *Letra Libre*.

Further copies of this booklet are available from:

Leeds Argentina Solidarity Group (LASG)
Cornerstone Resource Centre
16 Sholebroke Avenue
Leeds LS7 3HB
United Kingdom

email: paul_chatterton@yahoo.co.uk

ACKNOWLEDGEMENTS
Design Graphics Unit **Finance** School of Geography **Print** Butler and Tanner, Frome, Somerset. *Taking Back Control* is dedicated to all the inspirational people we met in Argentina — and those across the world — struggling for autonomy and a life without leaders or bosses. *¡La lucha sigue!*